pie·ography

If my life were a pie...

by

Jo Packham and The Publishers of Somerset Studio

Food Styling by: Anne Marie Klaske – Photography by: Traci Thorson

Quarry Books
100 Cummings Center, Suite 406L
Beverly, MA 01915

quarrybooks.com • craftside.typepad.com

makes one 8-inch x 8-inch book,
generously serves all

    1 production manager, Brandy Shay

    ½ art director, Matt Shay

    1 food stylist, Anne Marie Klaske

    1 photographer, Traci Thorson

    1 editor, Lisa Groen

    1 assistant editor, Patricia Nicolescu

    ¼ assistant editor, Sasha Troop

Combine all ingredients. Gently toss together. Let sit at least 1 hour or up to 99 days, depending on deadlines.

WARNING:

Baking in any type of canning jar is not recommend by the manufacturers and is done so at your own risk. Canning jars are designed to withstand hot water sterilization temperatures but run the risk of cracking when placed in a hot dry oven. (refer to Pie on page 17)

Every effort has been made to ensure that all of the information in this book is accurate. However, due to differing conditions, tools, and individual skills, the publisher, author, or contributors cannot be responsible for any injuries, losses, and other damages that may result from the use of the information in this book.

PRESS

215 Historic 25th Street, Ogen Utah

© 2012 Jo Packham

First published in the United States of America in 2013 by
Quarry Books, a member of
Quayside Publishing Group
100 Cummings Center
Suite 406-L
Beverly, Massachusetts 01915-6101
Telephone: (978) 282-9590
Fax: (978) 283-2742
www.quarrybooks.com

10 9 8 7 6 5 4 3 2 1

ISBN: 978-1-59253-853-9

Foreword

Everyone has a story to tell and even though we hear them and tell them every day we do not often think about them in a composition other than just that … a story with words and maybe images on a page. But what if it were more?

Pieography is a new design for storytelling. It is all about using ingredients to tell the story of someone's life and to share it not only in sight but in taste and smell.

Can you think of and tell the story of your life as a pie?

How do the ingredients that make the tale of your life combine to create a pie that is, in essence, the flavors and taste of your personal story? Is your life … and your pie … made simply with red apples grown in the neat, tended rows of a farmer's orchard? Or, is your pie — your life — more likely flavored with the essence of passion fruit, hinting at the exotic and the unknown? Yet still, it might be tinged with the au courant contradiction of salted caramel ice cream or its dark, rich sauce teeming with deep, complex flavors.

Pieography is not a book of memories of all that a much loved pie brings to mind because we each do have these remembered moments that are sweet or savory and filled with family and times not to be forgotten. No, this is something very different. "Pieography" is the biography of a woman's life told through the ingredients that create a slice — a taste — of her life in a pie. Savory, bitter, or richly appointed; simple and sweet, or messy and gooey, these pages tell her story through more than words.

Reading the stories on these pages of these women and then tasting their pies paints a picture for me that is as vivid as one that was created through the sonnets by Shakespeare and the prose by Oscar Wilde. They are real, they are emotional, and they are strong in ways other than the traditional, expected sight and sound. For the first time you can actually taste and smell the story that someone has to tell.

My mom told me a million stories of her life growing up. I didn't think about it at the time, but the pages of her story were written with the ingredients of her much loved and often made banana cream pie. Its crust was plain, yet the foundation of her life. She grew up with only a few basics of what was considered essential yet it made her stronger and uncomplicated. The rich creamy center was what she created for herself through her painting and her sewing to add "flavor," and color, and a softer richness to a stark reality. And the bananas were her exotic fruit that, even though grown in far off places that most of us only dream of, they have become so mainstream that even they are considered every day. The bananas were representative of her sewing of an ordinary wool skirt that could be worn to school or to work yet originated in her imagination with no pattern and from fabric that was once drapes that were no longer adequate to cover the living room windows or the wool blanket that had been discarded because of stains from careless use.

My mom and her life will never be forgotten, nor will her favored banana cream pie. In making her pie I celebrate her spirit, her style, her story, her life.

–Much love always, Jo

Dedication

ingredients...

Sweet Pies... continued

Jo Packham

Jo Packham, creator and Editor-in-Chief of *Where Women Cook*, has been a leading innovator in the handmade publishing market for more than 30 years. Her publishing company, WWC Press, is an imprint of Sterling Publishing. WWC Press also partners with Stampington & Company to produce the bestselling magazines *Where Women Cook—The Heart & Soul of Cooking*, *Where Women Create—Inspiring Work Spaces of Extraordinary Women*, and her newest publication, *Where Women Create BUSINESS—The Dream, The Reality, The Money, and The Success*.

Jo has personally authored the bestselling titles: *Where Women Create, Where Women Create: Book of Inspiration, Where Women Create: Book of Organization, Where Women Cook: CELEBRATE!*, and *Pieography: The Story of Your Life in a Pie*.

Her publishing company, Chapelle Ltd., has packaged more than 1,000 titles for most major publishers in the industry including: Oxmoor House, Meredith Corporation (Better Homes & Gardens), Rodale Press, and others.

In 2010, with Nancy Soriano, Jo co-founded THE CREATIVE CONNECTION—Women, Passion, Business.

You many visit her websites: www.wherewomencreate.com, www.wherewomencook.com, www.stampington.com, and www.thecreativeconnectionevent.com

My life as the ingredients to a pie ... what kind of a pie would that be? What would I taste like? What would the crust be made from? Would it be baked or would it be frozen? Would it be a healthy slice of life or a decadent guilty pleasure? Would there be just one pie ... or would there be more?

For me, as for each of you, more than one pie is needed to tell the stories of our lives and I believe that there is no other way to begin than with a pie for each meal of the day: a breakfast pie, created like the rich, romantic, foreign French quiche; a nontraditional Italian inspired pizza pie for lunch; and a substantial English shepherd's pie for dinner. Each pie, for each meal, must be a foundation on which to build. Each is based on solid traditions, yet inspiring in their content and in their presentation—because nothing about my life, or my pies, can be considered classical or conventional.

Each of these pies must be made from the freshest garden ingredients because my day-to-day life must be filled with all that is good and fresh and new. Each pie, representative of my creative soul, is abundant in texture and color as are the variety of heirloom tomatoes I always use because their reds, yellows, oranges, and greens offer a feast for the eyes as much as they do for the palette. Each must be touched with subtle herbs like oregano and dusted with the slightest hint of sea salt and fresh ground pepper because, like my life, there must be subtle hints of something extra.

My pies must always have fine aged cheese for flavor because I cannot imagine many of my recipes, or my life, not touched by a strong essence of wisdom that comes with age. Each pie must be made and served individually because, again, in my life everything must be given exclusively, distinctively, and creatively because there is only you as you stand by yourself. Each of my family and friends must be honored and respected as the individual that she once was, as well as the one that she has become, and the woman she dreams of in her future.

Individual Spinach Quiche

makes eight individual quiches from jumbo muffin pan

1 onion, diced small

½ lb. fresh small mushrooms, quartered

Butter

2 sheets puff pastry, defrosted, rolled out lightly and each sheet cut into 4 squares

5 large eggs

Sea salt and freshly cracked black pepper

⅔ cup milk

1 lb. fresh spinach

½ lb. variety of heirloom tomatoes, quartered

¼ lb. feta cheese, crumbled

3 TB. freshly grated Parmesan or Romano cheese

1. Preheat oven to 375°F.

2. Cook onion and mushrooms in 2 tablespoons of butter until slightly brown and tender.

3. Butter extra-large muffin cups, or small quiche dishes. Place a square of puff pastry into each muffin cup or dish, and fold the edges down so they are even with top of each muffin cup or dish.

4. Whisk eggs together in bowl and add pinch of sea salt and a little cracked pepper. Stir in spinach, mushrooms, onion, tomatoes, and feta cheese.

5. Pour mixture into muffin cups or quiche dishes. Sprinkle with the Parmesan or Romano cheese.

6. Cook for about 30 minutes. Check to make certain knife comes out clean when inserted in middle of quiche.

7. Serve immediately. Makes a delightful luncheon with tomato slices lightly sprinkled with sea salt and cracked pepper, fresh Parmesan or Romano cheese, and a glass of red wine.

Individual Heirloom Tomato Pizzas

makes four 7-inch individual pizzas

Pizza Crust

- 1½ tsp. active dry yeast
- 1 tsp. sugar
- ¾ cup warm water
- 1 cup cake flour
- 1 cup + 3 TB. all-purpose flour
- 1¼ tsp. kosher salt
- 1 TB. olive oil

1. In small bowl, whisk together yeast, sugar, and warm water. Let stand 5 minutes.

2. Using food processor, combine cake flour and all-purpose flour with kosher salt. Pulse 5–6 times.

3. Add 1 tablespoon of olive oil into yeast mixture, whisk well. While motor is running, slowly add yeast mixture into flour mixture until all is combined.

4. Pulse 12 more times to knead dough. You will be done with dough when it cleans the inside of bowl and is still slightly sticky.

5. Form dough into a ball and place into lightly greased large bowl. Cover tightly with plastic wrap and let dough rise until doubled in size, 1 hour. Divide dough into four equal sections and shape into balls. Roll out each dough ball into a 7" circle.

Pizza Toppings and Assembly

- 1 batch of pizza crust
- Olive oil
- 10 oz. mozzarella cheese, grated
- ½ pint of small heirloom tomatoes in a variety of colors, halved or quartered if large
- Sea salt and freshly cracked black pepper

1. Preheat oven to 425°F.

2. Place each pizza round onto pizza stone (or well seasoned baking sheet). Brush 2 teaspoons of olive oil onto each pizza round.

3. Add cheese evenly to each pizza round, leaving a ½" border around outside.

4. Place heirloom tomatoes over cheese and season with sea salt and cracked pepper.

5. Bake for about 10–12 minutes (or until crust is golden brown).

6. Drizzle reduced balsamic glaze over each individual pizza.

Reduced Balsamic Glaze

- 2 cups balsamic vinegar

1. Pour vinegar into heavy saucepan and bring to a simmer. Turn heat to low and reduce vinegar for 30 minutes, or until vinegar becomes thick enough to coat back of spoon. You will end up with ½ cup.

2. Remove from heat and cool.

3. Pour into an airtight container and store at either room temperature or in refrigerator. If you do store glaze in refrigerator, don't be alarmed if it hardens up a bit. Simply place container into mug of warm water and it will soften quickly.

Individual Shepherd's Pie

makes eight individual 10-ounce pies

Pie Filling

  1 lb. boneless tender prime rib, cut into 1-inch cubes
     Coarse sea salt and freshly cracked black pepper
     All-purpose unbleached flour
  3 TB. olive oil, divided
  1 cup onions, chopped
  1 lb. small mushrooms, cleaned, cut into quarters
  ½ cup red wine
1½ cups beef stock or leftover gravy
  2 garlic cloves, minced and separated into 2 piles
  1 TB. fresh oregano
  1 lb. small heirloom tomatoes, cut into quarters
     (use variety of colors)
  6 ears fresh white sweet corn, removed from cob
  ½ lb. fresh sweet peas
  1 small bundle asparagus (about 18 small spears),
     washed and cut into 2-inch lengths

1. Sprinkle beef generously with sea salt and cracked pepper, then dust with flour to coat.

2. Heat 2 tablespoons oil in same pot over medium-high heat. Add half of beef. Sauté until browned. Transfer beef to large bowl.

3. Repeat with 2 tablespoons oil and remaining beef. Add 1 more tablespoon oil to same pot, if needed.

4. Add onions and mushrooms. Cover and cook over medium-low heat until very tender, about 10 minutes (bottom of pot will be very dark).

5. Add wine to pot. Increase heat and boil until wine evaporates, scraping up browned bits, about 5 minutes.

6. Add stock (or gravy), 1 chopped garlic clove, and oregano. Bring to boil.

7. Add beef with any accumulated juices. Cover, reduce heat to low, and simmer 1 hour.

8. Stir in tomatoes, corn, peas, and asparagus. Simmer 5 minutes. Season with sea salt and cracked pepper.

9. Transfer to small baking containers. (I used 10 ounce custard cups, or you can use a large muffin pan.)

10. Preheat oven to 375°F.

Pie Topping

1¼ lbs. russet potatoes, peeled, cut into 1-inch cubes
  2 TB. unsalted butter
  2 TB. extra virgin olive oil
  1 cup half and half
  ¼ cup bottled horseradish, drained
1¼ cups Kasseri cheese, coarsely grated , divided
     (Romano can be used)

1. Cook potatoes in large pot boiling salted water until tender, about 18 minutes.

2. Meanwhile, melt butter and oil in medium saucepan over medium-high heat.

3. Add garlic. Sauté until fragrant, about 1 minute. Add half and half, bring to simmer.

4. Drain potatoes. Return to pot. Stir over medium heat until excess moisture evaporates.

5. Add half and half mixture, horseradish, and mash potatoes until smooth. Stir in ¾ cup of cheese. Season with sea salt and cracked pepper.

6. Drop potatoes over filling by heaping tablespoons, covering filling completely. Sprinkle with cheese.

7. Bake pies until filling is heated through and topping is golden, about 45 minutes.

14

However, the true essence of my life in a pie has to be one created for dessert and made from passion fruit with a thick, rich, crunchy macadamia nut crust and topped with all of my favorite "guilty pleasures." It only makes sense, doesn't it? Everything about my pie, like my life, has to be exotic, rich, complicated, expensive, unexpected, bitter, sweet, and created to be served in something memorable. Can you even imagine me with a homemade apple pie baked in a traditional pie pan served with vanilla ice cream?

After all, what other fruit is more indicative of me as an entrepreneurial, creative soul than passion fruit? In one word, it says "everything" that I am ... all consumed, ardent, impatient, insatiable, impulsive, intense, unpredictable, and devoted! Passionate: yes; nutty: absolutely; exotic: *mais oui*; unexpected: of course; over-the-top: always; but my life has also tasted the long-lasting, sweet texture of coconut; the bitter taste of natural, raw, dark chocolate; the rich, thick, creamy experiences of real heavy cream; the new, hip, unexpected flavor of salted caramel; and the childhood innocence of popcorn.

My life is also somewhat like a true French caramel sauce—the French cook their caramel longer, to a dark copper color, not the light golden browns of the chefs in the U.S. This is the Frenchman's secret to great caramel and my secret to a great life: the light golden browns just taste sweet and sticky, but the dark ones are nutty, rich, complex, with a trace of bitterness.

For me, the ingredients have to be abundant and the best of the best. Why would you include fat-free whipping cream and cheat yourself of the richness of heavy hand-whipped cream flavored with exotic fruits or spices, simply to save a few calories? These are the tastes that become the threads that you use to weave your life; you can either use the best and be the best, or you can use less and be less.

And for the serving of my pies and the living of my life, one pie would never be enough. You must make too many pies for everyone and serve them so that they take your breath away from the first minute you see them, and everyone must have at least three.

I LOVE my over-abundant life, the very bitter of it that makes me wonder if it is all really worth it, and the very sweet of it that brings tears to my eyes with each taste and with every memory.

Coconut Macadamia Nut Pie with Passion Fruit Cream, Salted Caramel Drizzle & Dark Chocolate Popcorn Sprinkles

makes ten 8-ounce glass jars

WARNING:
Baking in any type of canning jar is not recommend by the manufacturers and is done so at your own risk. Canning jars are designed to withstand hot water sterilization temperatures but run the risk of cracking when placed in a hot dry oven.

Dark Chocolate Popcorn Sprinkles

- 6 cups popcorn, popped
- ¼ cup sugar
- ¼ cup light corn syrup
- 2 TB. unsalted butter
- ⅛ cup unsweetened cocoa powder
- ½ tsp. coarse sea salt

1. Preheat oven to 200°F.

2. Put popcorn in large bowl.

3. Put sugar, corn syrup, butter, cocoa, and salt in medium saucepan. Cook over medium heat, stirring, until mixture comes to gentle simmer, about 5 minutes.

4. Pour sugar mixture over popcorn, toss to coat.

5. Transfer to rimmed baking sheets; bake, stirring every 20 minutes, until almost dry, about 1 hour.

6. Let cool on sheets on wire racks.

7. Break popcorn pieces apart and set aside.

8. Sprinkle popcorn over salted caramel sauce when ready to serve.

Continued on next page…

17

Crunchy Nut Crust

    1 cup macadamia nuts
    3¼ cups graham cracker crumbs (about 30 crackers)
    1 TB. sugar
    1 cup (2 sticks) unsalted butter, melted
    Pinch of salt

1. Preheat oven to 325°F.
2. Spread macadamia nuts onto a baking sheet and toast for 7–9 minutes or until golden brown. Let cool, coarsely chop.
3. In large bowl, thoroughly mix together nuts, graham cracker cumbs, sugar, butter, and salt.
4. Spray glass jar with non-stick cooking spray.
5. Press nut crust mixture evenly into bottom and partially up sides of jar. Crust should be ¼"–½" thick.

Pie Filling

    ⅔ cup sugar
    2 large eggs
    2 large egg yolks
    1⅓ cup real whipping cream, divided
    1 cup coconut flakes

1. Whisk sugar, eggs, and egg yolks in large bowl for 1 minute.
2. Stir in whipping cream and coconut.
3. Fill small jars about half full.
4. Bake until set in center. (Baking time depends on size of jar … check after 5 minutes.)
5. Let cool and refrigerate until needed.

Passion Fruit Cream

    1½ cups whipping cream, chilled
    1 cup sugar
    ⅔ cup sour cream
    10 TB. passion fruit pulp or puree

1. Whisk cream, sugar, and sour cream until stiff peaks form.
2. Gently fold in fruit pulp or puree. Set aside in refrigerator while preparing caramel sauce.
3. Dollop on top of tarts immediately before serving.

Deep, Dark, Salted Butter Caramel Sauce
(Sauce au Caramel au Beurre Salé)

makes about 1⅓ cups

    1 cup sugar
    6 TB. salted butter
    ½ cup + 2 TB. heavy cream, at room temperature

1. Melt sugar over medium to moderately high heat in large pot (2–3 quarts). Continually stir sugar as it melts to ensure even melting. Cook liquid sugar to dark copper color.
2. Add butter all at once, stir until melted.
3. Pour in heavy cream. (The cream will cause mixture to foam.)
4. Stir or whisk to smooth sauce consistency.
5. Put 1 scoop of passion fruit cream on each individual pie.
6. Drizzle caramel over pie.
Note: Caramel sauce may be saved until later by pouring mixture into a jar and storing in refrigerator for up to 2 weeks. It will thicken during storage, so heat in microwave for about 60 seconds for proper consistency. (Test your microwave; each heats differently.)
7. Sprinkle popcorn on top, serve immediately.

Savory

MADALINA ANDRONIC

Madalina Andronic is a young Romanian artist, working freelance after finishing an MA at University of the Arts London, where she specialized in illustration. She has produced work for magazines, online media, design studios, and advertising agencies, and has illustrated albums worldwide. She's also just published her first illustrated children's book *Fairy of Dawn*, inspired by Romanian folklore, and already has an idea for the next one.

Illustration is her speciality and what she enjoys doing most, yet she is definitely an illustrator who cooks and who can wholeheartedly say that sometimes she dreams of being a chic chef in an even more chic French bistro, serving *pain au chocolat* to her very chic clients.

Madalina lives in Bucharest, Romania, and shares her studio with her boyfriend, Claudiu, who is also an artist. Together they are trying to set up an arts and crafts studio with a complex range of handmade designs.

Madalina developed a keen interest in fairytales, folklore, reindeers, and Dutch architecture, alongside a recently discovered affinity for pottery and textile design. She considers herself privileged and lucky to be doing a job she loves. Madalina's lovely art can be admired at www.madiandronic.com or www.de-adevaratelea.blogspot.com.

Some may say that I'm a complicated woman, but when it comes to my creative process, I like to keep it simple and traditional. As an artist, my illustrations may pop and glow with color and details, yet the ideas behind them always speak about the simple things in life and enjoying life as it is. I am finally having an honest, fuss-free relationship with myself and with my loved ones. So if I were to take all of these ingredients to the kitchen and translate them into a pie, I believe the result would be the most simple, hearty cheese pie. This pie not only reflects my feelings and my attitude, but it also speaks to my love of the traditional side of art and life. The cheese pie is one of Romania's traditional signature dishes. But my pie is creamier and fluffier than my great-grandmothers' crumbly version. It melts in your mouth and makes you wonder how a "not-so-much-love-at-first-sight" pie could leave such an impression.

I start by choosing the cheeses. I select a soft, milky, slightly salted Romanian cow's cheese, then the textured cottage cheese, plus the fluffy, dreamy cream cheese. I add the farm fresh eggs and there it is: my perfect pie filling. Somehow, this egg-cheese mixture brings back the taste of my childhood, when my favorite thing to eat was a fat slice of cheese dipped in a soft-cooked egg yolk. For me, this pie is the most genuine and delicious souvenir from that time.

I choose not to have a dainty, decorated single crust pie, since I'm not always a fan of discipline and order, so I roll up my savory memories in a thin, silky pastry and arrange them like toy soldiers on a baking tray. The whisked egg and yogurt mixture, poured on top, is my simple, quick way of softening an otherwise rough version of the traditional cheese pie—making it like my fluffiest memories. And last but not least, I'll enjoy a slice of my pie with a simple glass of sour yogurt for a bubbly pinch of freshness.

Madi's Hale & Hearty Cheese Pie

makes one 13x19-inch baking dish, or two 9-inch pies

Pie Pastry

1 package filo pastry

Pie Filling

2 eggs
1 cup salty cow's cheese, grated
1 cup cottage cheese
2 TB. cream cheese

Pie Topping and Assembly

1 egg
½ cup plain Greek/creamy yogurt

1. Preheat oven to 370°F.

2. For filling, combine 2 eggs and cheese, mixing well, until creamy. Make sure there are no lumps, as they won't melt during baking and they will give your pie a dry texture.

3. Roll out 2 layers of filo pastry on a clean surface. Spread 2–3 tablespoons of cheese filling on top of pastry and carefully roll up cheese in filo. Place roll on baking tray lined with parchment paper. Repeat process with remaining filo, making sure to use two sheets of pastry for each cheese roll.

4. After pie rolls are placed on tray, whip remaining 1 egg with yogurt and pour mixture on top of pie rolls, spreading evenly with brush. Place pie rolls in oven and let bake for 35 minutes, or until golden. Serve while hot with a glass of yogurt.

DYAN CARLSON

Dyan Carlson is a graduate of L'Academie de Cuisine where she studied culinary arts under Chefs Francois and Pascal Dionot. She also studied pastry making with former White House pastry chef Roland Mesnier. Her internship under Chef Jeffrey Buben at the Occidental Restaurant in Washington, D.C., was, in her words, "The most grueling and intense year of my life. It almost broke me. However, I am successful today because of the time that Chef Buben took with me all of those years ago. I would do it all over again."

Dyan also worked with Chef Michel Richard at the Baltimore Citronelle. Of the experience, she says, "Chef Richard was one of the most patient chefs with whom I have worked. He would stop anything he was doing to show me something, to teach me."

Currently living in Charlottesville, Virginia, Dyan works as a freelance food writer. She has written for publications such as *Organic Producer, Edible Chesapeake, Edible Blue Ridge*, and *Flavor Magazine*. She also works for Whole Foods Market, where she teaches cooking classes.

Every ingredient in my Heirloom Tomato and Goat Cheese Pie says something about me: who I am, where I come from, and what I have learned. And what a life it is! The nerdy fat girl from Baltimore breaks out of her shell, attends a French cooking school, and goes on to work with noted chefs—including Jeffrey Buben and Michel Richard. She embraces the unconventional beauty that she was given, flaunts her curves, opens her heart, and meets the man of her dreams who fills her life with laughter, love, and hope.

Just like me: the perfect pie crust is shaped by patience and perseverance. It's strong but tender. Flakiness is expected and encouraged, even if it means adding in a bit more fat. Overworking a pie crust makes it hard and tough.

Heirloom tomatoes do not conform to society's idea of perfection and beauty, and yet they are highly sought after for their unusual shape, colors, and flavors. An understanding of their history is an important aspect to their popularity and essential to their successful growth.

Basil, fresh from the garden, tells you exactly what it is at first glance and its fragrance reminds us of warm summer nights.

White and unassuming, often thought to be bland, creamy goat's cheese often surprises with its peppery tartness. Many people make a sour face at first, but warm up once they acquire a taste for the unusual.

Delicate and fruity olive oil, often assumed to be foreign and expensive, has the ability to withstand high heat without breaking down. Once people become familiar with the oil, they insist on having it in their kitchen.

Herbes de Provence and Dijon mustard are basic staples of French cooking. Their earthy flavors make most people wonder, "Just what is in this?"

To enjoy this pie best, sit outside on a warm summer night, surrounded by friends and fireflies. Though this pie could stand alone, it is best served warm with a salad of peppery greens dressed in a delicate vinaigrette. Strawberries, still warm from the sun, and slices of ice-cold watermelon might stand by, ready for dessert. A chilled glass of Sauvignon Blanc or ice-cold Southern sweet tea completes the menu.

25

Heirloom Tomato & Goat Cheese Pie

makes two 10-inch tarts

Traditional Pâte Brisée (pie crust)

    2½ cups all-purpose flour

    ½ tsp. salt

    1 cup cold butter

    ⅓ cup cold water

1. In small bowl, mix together flour and salt.

2. Using pastry cutter, cut chilled butter into flour until it resembles coarse sand with a few pea-sized chunks of butter still visible.

3. Sprinkle water evenly over mixture and toss gently a few times, just until it forms a ball that holds together.

4. Separate dough into 2 balls. Flatten slightly into thick disk shapes, wrap in plastic. Chill for several hours before working with it.

Pie Topping and Assembly

    3 TB. Dijon mustard

    6 oz. goat cheese, crumbled

    8 oz. yellow pear or grape tomatoes, sliced (or quartered for a more rustic look)

    1 tsp. Herbes de Provence

    3 fresh basil leaves, chopped chiffonade (reserve a few strips for garnish)

    ¼ tsp. freshly cracked black pepper

    2 oz. extra virgin olive oil

    ¼ tsp. black truffle salt (if not available, regular sea salt will do just fine)

1. Preheat oven to 375°F.

2. Grease tart pan and put in crust.

3. Bake pie crust for 10 minutes (fill pie with dried beans, do not poke holes in crust). Let cool for 5 minutes.

4. Spread bottom of crust with mustard, sprinkle with half of cheese, arrange tomato slices.

5. Sprinkle on remaining cheese.

6. Sprinkle with Herbes, basil leave, pepper, and drizzle on olive oil.

7. Bake for about 30 minutes.

8. Remove from oven, garnish with strips of basil, and sprinkle on truffle salt.

9. Serve warm or at room temperature.

26

Tip: Let dough rest, if possible, overnight in the refrigerator. When ready to use, remove from fridge for about 30 minutes before rolling. Be sure to handle dough gently.

27

Sarah Spry Keenan

Chef Sarah Spry Keenan, co-owner at Whole Health Everyday, is a noted graduate of Laguna Culinary Arts Professional Chef Program. An avid foodie, blogger, and passionate chef, Sarah's first love is Thai cuisine—which she has prepared for more than twenty years. She continues to study this regional food and brings all the flavor and health benefits of Thai food into her cooking at every opportunity.

Raised by a family "full of hardcore health food freaks," Sarah was fed the purest and freshest foods as a child. Her grandmother had a huge garden, chickens, and goats. Both her mother and grandmother owned health food stores. Growing up in California, Sarah often stopped with her family at roadside fruit stands to pick up snacks. She has always had a relationship with good, fresh food.

Sarah spent time as a pastry chef at the renowned Ahwahnee Hotel, in Yosemite National Park. She continues to pursue a full-rounded exploration of all food and its presentation. She is the Sous Chef at Casa Laguna, www.casalaguna.com.

To read more about Sarah's work, visit wholehealtheveryday.com and spryonfood.com.

There's the old adage that "a picture is worth a thousand words." Ah, but FOOD … well, food speaks to all our senses. We derive pleasure from the sight of food; the smell of food; the sounds of chopping, popping, and sizzling; from the warmth that emanates from a hot dish; and, of course, our taste buds relish the flavor of a well-prepared meal. In the same way that food speaks to our senses, it can tell us a lot about the person who created it. Take my Lobster Potpie, for instance. In its ingredients, its construction, and its flavors, you will find a story about me, Chef Sarah.

When you smell a potpie cooking, what do you think of? Warmth, nourishment, and family—all baked up in a rich and savory sauce. These are the reasons I started making potpies many years ago. For much longer than I've been a chef, I've been a wife and a mother. I was always looking for nutritious and filling foods that would appeal to my husband and son. I could serve the pies up fresh, or make them ahead of time and freeze them. When my family had them for dinner in my absence, I was there in spirit: a warm and loving presence in pie form.

Family is my first passion, but you can see a progression of my personality and other passions in the rest of the recipe for Lobster Potpie. The puff pastry crust, for instance, puts a modern twist on the traditional potpie. It is also crispy and flaky (read into those personality traits what you will) and its golden glaze attests to my love of butter. Lobster represents my great love of the ocean and beaches (my husband has even trapped Pacific lobsters off the coast of Dana Point, very near where we live), but also my appreciation for fine dining. Oh, and we all know about lobster and butter … did I mention I love butter? The veggies I use are fresh and fragrant and shine in their own right; I'd like to think I do the same. Finish off the sauce with Pernod (let's call it refined and pungent—in a good way).

My many passions went into my Lobster Potpie recipe, and that love shines through in its rich, buttery goodness. I first concocted this dish while in culinary school when I was handed a live lobster and given two hours to create something fantastic. I achieved a perfect score, but better yet, almost brought my French instructor to tears.

Yes, food tells stories to all of our senses, and the Lobster Potpie has a pieography to convey. The words I've used are only the beginning of what the pie has to say about Chef Sarah: warm, nourishing, traditional yet modern, crispy and flaky, fresh, refined. I am complex like the blending of textures and flavors in this entrée, and the story this pie paints … is a picture of me.

Lobster Potpies in Puff Pastry Cups

makes six 4-inch pies

Pie Topping

- 3 cups fumet/fish stock
- 2–3 fresh lobster tails, yielding 1 lb. of meat
- 1 cup frozen peas
- 1½ cups leeks, dice small
- 1 cup fennel, dice small
- 1 cup celery, dice small
- 8 TB. unsalted butter, divided
- ⅓ cup all-purpose flour
- 3 TB. Pernod
- Salt and pepper
- ¼ cup flat leaf parsley, finely chopped + sprigs
- 3 sheets frozen puff pastry, 9" x 9" each
- 1 egg, for egg wash

1. Simmer fumet/stock in large saucepot, add lobster tails, and cook for 7–8 minutes. Remove tails and let cool, remove shells.

2. Add shells back to simmering stock. Simmer on low for about 20 minutes. Strain stock and reserve.

3. Chop lobster meat in small chunks. Place in mixing bowl, add frozen peas, set aside.

4. Sauté leeks, fennel, and celery with 6 tablespoons of butter in a large sauce pan on medium heat until they are translucent, 8–10 minutes.

5. Add flour and cook on low heat for 5 more minutes, stirring occasionally to cook out flour flavor.

6. Deglaze pan with Pernod. Be careful, this may flame up.

7. Slowly add stock, 1 cup at a time. Simmer for 5 minutes to cook out alcohol.

8. Add last 2 tablespoons of butter. Season with salt and pepper to taste, add chopped parsley.

9. Pour sauce over lobster and pea mixture, and taste for proper seasoning. Keep warm and set aside.

Puff Pastry Cups (Vol au Vent) and Assembly

1. Preheat oven to 425°F.

2. Slightly thaw sheets of frozen puff pastry, not too much, just enough to cut dough.

3. Using a 4" and 3" round pastry cutter, cut twelve 4" circles from dough. Take 6 rounds and cut 3" rounds, leaving a small ring of dough. Place this on top of other six 4" rounds. Place in freezer for 10–15 minutes on parchment lined baking sheet.

4. Egg wash each one and bake for 15–20 minutes until golden brown. They should puff up into pastry cups. Push middle down if it pops up, and fill with lobster mixture.

5. Garnish with parsley sprigs. Serve at once.

Anne Marie Klaske

When Anne Marie Klaske and her carpenter husband moved to their farm in the country, they restored not only their neglected 1920s farmhouse, but turned the lawn into pastures, a large family kitchen garden, and restored three acres into Illinois prairie. In the prairie, you'll find their heritage chickens roaming, along with rescued horses grazing. You'll hear Anne Marie's husband's bees humming in their hives, and six children creating childhood memories.

Raised with traditional values in and out of the kitchen, Anne Marie is aware of the meaning of fresh and real food. The meals she prepares for her family, friends, and guests are fresh, real, and traditional farm style. Her home, farm, and recipes can be found in *Midwest Living* magazine, *Where Women Cook*, the bestselling book *Romantic Prairie Style*, and its companion *Romantic Prairie Style Cookbook*.

With constant devotion and gratitude to God, Anne Marie embraces her freedom on the farm while striving for more self-sustainability. Encouraging others to tie on their aprons or grab their gardening gloves, she blogs online about her life of cooking from scratch, baking, mothering, home schooling, farm animals, sewing, and faith. To help support local artists and shop owners, Anne Marie and husband Jason open their farm to welcome over 4,000 visitors each year to art classes and story-like barn sales.

 32

Visit Anne Marie online at www.nadafarmlife.org.

My life & Traditional Rustic Chicken Potpie

Instead of seeking complex items from other parts of the world, I dig deeply into the root cellar to find harvested items that come together comfortably. It doesn't take 30 minutes to prepare and throw my pie in the oven. My pie, my life, is a traditional dish that, in order to taste really good, requires a dedication to the freshest ingredients. I let them harmoniously blend together in order to completely satisfy others and myself.

My traditional rustic potpie is not about one key ingredient or taste, rather, it's a complex blend of simple, choice ingredients that create a rustic exterior that satisfies in even a small slice. Most important in my life are family, friends, and our experiences together. I would not be who I am, and my pie wouldn't taste quite like it does, if it weren't for my loved ones. Their flavors are blended with mine. All of this together creates my pie, my life. Instead of store-bought crust and already diced carrots, I make everything from scratch—raw. Nothing is uniform or perfect.

The six souls who live from the substance of this pie are shown how to make it and the ingredients I have used to create it. In time, they will eventually make their own pies, each one being unique. A rustic golden and slightly sea-salted crust blankets the inside, keeping it warm and ready to share with others. In time, it will eventually be completely gone, and God willing, it will be a pie that will be remembered and cherished from the inside. What is inside the pie is ultimately more important than how it appears on the outside.

Traditional Rustic Chicken Potpie
makes one 15-inch deep dish pie, or two 9-inch pies

Rustic Pastry

  3 cups all-purpose flour
    Sea salt and freshly cracked black pepper
  1 tsp. baking powder
  ½ cup pure vegetable shortening
  8 TB. sweet cream/unsalted butter, diced
  1 cup ice water (approximately)
  1 egg beaten with 1 TB. water, for egg wash

1. Preheat oven to 375°F.

2. For pastry, you can use a food processor, mixer, or do it by hand (which I did): Mix flour, sea salt, and baking powder in large mixing bowl. Cut up shortening and butter into small pieces, and with pastry cutter, mix completely until dough is size of peas. Add ice water 1 tablespoon at a time (you may not need a whole cup of water), turning flour mixture with fork, until all flour is moistened and dough comes together into a ball.

3. Knead 3–4 times onto floured board and roll out pastry to fit over sides of desired pie pan(s). (If baking only one pie, now is your chance to wrap 1 pie crust tightly and freeze for later use.)

Pie Filling

  5 chicken breasts
    Olive oil
    Sea salt and freshly cracked black pepper
 12 TB. (1½ sticks) unsalted butter
 1½ cups Vidalia (or yellow) onions, finely chopped
  3 cups rich chicken stock
  ¾ cup all-purpose unbleached flour
  ¼ cup cream (whipping cream is fine)
  2 cups carrots, sliced and blanched
  2 cups peas
 1½ cups fresh mushrooms, sliced (sauté in butter until golden on edges)

1. Preheat oven to 350°F.

2. Cut off all fat from chicken breasts, wash, and pat dry.

3. Place chicken breasts onto baking sheet. Drizzle and rub olive oil onto both sides of chicken breasts, as well as a sprinkle of sea salt and cracked pepper to taste.

4. Bake in oven for about 30 minutes, or until cooked through. Remove from oven and let cool enough to handle, and then cut chicken into rustic bite size pieces. Depending on size of chicken breasts, you may have some left over. You need about 5 cups of ckicken pieces in recipe, so save any leftover chicken for a quick addition to tomorrow's lunch salad.

5. Melt butter in medium cast iron skillet (or pan of your choice) and add onions. Sauté until translucent.

6. Meanwhile, heat chicken stock (if you need to make your chicken stock more "rich" in flavor, add a few chicken bouillon cubes).

7. Add flour into butter/onion mixture and stir constantly for 1 minute. Add chicken stock, stir constantly, and let simmer 1 minute (or until stock becomes thick).

8. Add cream, cubed chicken, carrots, peas, and mushrooms. Thoroughly combine all goodness! Put chicken/vegetable mixture into desired pan. (I used a 15" round stoneware deep dish pie pan but two 9" pie pans work will work as well.) Cover mixture with pastry, letting it hang-over edges of pie pan(s).

9. Brush outside of pie with egg wash and make a delightful design with knife (or just cut slits) on top. Optional: sprinkle a bit of sea salt and cracked pepper on top of pie before baking.

10. Place in oven for 1 hour, or if cooking in conventional oven, 40 minutes. You will know pie is done when filling is bubbling and smells good.

11. Serve pie with side of fresh salad or homemade applesauce, and if you are the proper age, a good stout beer. Enjoy!

ANDREA MEYERS

Andrea Meyers is a recipe developer and photographer in Northern Virginia, and she has been cooking and photographing her way around the world for over 20 years. She spent eight years teaching abroad in the Pacific, South America, and the Middle East and recorded her memories of all the places she lived and visited on film. Now she has combined her passion for making memorable images with her passion for beautiful and delicious food. Her recipes have been featured in the books *Where Women Cook Celebrate!*, *One Big Table*, and *Good Bite Weeknight Meals: Delicious Made Easy*, and she has been featured in videos for GoodBite.com, The Real Women of Philadelphia, The Life Well Laughed Project, Moovision.com, and BettyCrocker.com.

When not in her own kitchen making bread and other baked goods from scratch, or cooking a meal with fresh vegetables and herbs from the family garden, Andrea can be found traveling throughout Northern Virginia photographing farms and vineyards.

Visit Andrea at www.andreameyers.com and www.andreasrecipes.com.

My soul is tied to the seasons and the earth, so the flavors in my pie must be warm, earthy, and savory, with fresh vegetables and herbs that my family and I grow in our garden. There's nothing like pulling your own carrots, parsnips, and celery root out of the ground for the first time, or going out to the garden to snip parsley, sage, thyme, and rosemary whenever you need it. I have an overwhelming satisfaction every time I cook with our homegrown food. By carrying on my family's traditions, I feel I'm making my mother, grandmothers, and great-grandmothers proud.

As a photographer, I'm also drawn to the land. I've recently begun telling the stories of local Virginia farms, gardens, and vineyards through pictures. I visit them seasonally, capturing their crops in their dormancy, infancy, maturity, and harvest.

So my pie must be a harvest potpie, a simple meal of chicken, vegetables, herbs, and pie crust.

I adore this recipe because it's perfect for using leftover roasted chicken (or turkey), and for including so many fresh vegetables and herbs from the garden. In an old casserole dish, a puff pastry poofs magically in the oven, with buttery crisp layers atop the warm, homey filling. On a cool, late autumn evening with my family, with a fire roaring nearby, I dish this meal into vintage bowls to eat at a rustic table.

Harvest Potpie with Chicken, Carrots, Parsnips, Celery Root, Sweet Potatoes, & Garden-Fresh Herbs

makes one 2-quart casserole dish

1 celery root, peeled and diced

1 large carrot, peeled and diced

1 large parsnip, peeled and diced

1 medium sweet potato, peeled and diced

4 TB. olive oil

4 sprigs fresh thyme

3 inch sprig fresh rosemary, cut into thirds

3 TB. unsalted butter

3 shallots, peeled and thinly sliced

⅛ tsp. freshly cracked black pepper

2 leaves fresh sage, minced

3 TB. unbleached all-purpose flour

1 cup homemade chicken stock

1 lb. roasted chicken meat (white, dark, or mixed), diced

1¾ cups half and half, room temperature

½ cup frozen peas, thawed

3 TB. fresh parsley, chopped

1 sheet frozen puff pastry, thawed

1 egg white + 1 TB. water

1. Move oven rack to middle and preheat oven to 400°F.

2. Line 9" x 13" baking pan with foil, and fill with diced celery root, carrot, parsnip, and sweet potato. Toss with olive oil, and lay 2 sprigs of fresh thyme and 2 pieces of rosemary on top. Roast in oven until vegetables are fork tender, but not mushy, about 25 minutes. Remove from oven.

3. In 4-quart saucepan, melt butter over medium heat. Add shallots and cook, stirring, until shallots are soft and glistening, about 5 minutes. Add cracked pepper and minced sage. Mince remaining rosemary and add to shallots, remove leaves from remaining sprigs of thyme, and add to shallots. Stir and allow herbs to release their fragrance, about 2 minutes.

4. Whisk in flour and continue to cook while stirring, until flour takes on slightly nutty flavor, about 5 minutes. Slowly whisk in chicken stock until it fully combines with flour and shallots, then stir in half and half. Continue cooking until sauce starts to thicken, about 10 minutes.

5. Stir in diced chicken, roasted vegetables, and thawed peas. Cook until all ingredients are warmed through, about 5 minutes. Stir in parsley, then cover to keep warm. Lightly grease a 2-quart casserole dish.

6. Dust a cutting board lightly with flour and roll out puff pastry until it's about 1" longer and wider than casserole dish. Use mini autumn leaf cutters to cut three or four leaves out of top of puff pastry, if desired, and set aside. Pour chicken filling into casserole dish, then carefully lift puff pastry and lay it on top of casserole. Trim corners if necessary so pastry is even all the way around. Press pastry to edge of dish to seal. Lay leaves on pastry for decoration, if desired, then use a pastry brush to brush egg white wash all over pastry.

7. Bake in preheated oven until pastry is brown and puffy and filling is bubbly, about 30 minutes. Remove from oven and allow to rest about 5–10 minutes before serving.

BETH PRICE

Beth Price is the director of recipe testing for Leite's Culinaria, a James Beard award-winning food blog. She also develops and styles recipes for *The Local Palate*, a new magazine covering the food culture of the South, and is a contributor to *Where Women Cook*.

Beth began her culinary career as an intern for celebrity chef Nathalie Dupree. Under her tutelage, she learned to develop, edit, and test recipes for publication in cookbooks, magazines, food blogs, and newspapers. Her original recipes have appeared in the *Post and Courier*, *The Local Palate*, and the soon-to-be-published *Mastering the Art of Southern Cooking*, by Nathalie Dupree and Cynthia Graubart. She is a member of the International Association of Culinary Professionals, Slow Food International, and is involved with the James Beard Foundation.

When she is not in the kitchen, you can find her working as a background actor on the set of *Army Wives*, shot in her hometown of Charleston, South Carolina. She divides her time between Charleston and the Caribbean, and her food philosophy reflects the melding of Southern and island flavors. She can be reached at beth.leitesculinaria@gmail.com.

Who am I? I am a wife, a mother, and a cook. I am a Southerner with long ties to Bermuda. I am a traditionalist and a modernist. I am lavishly decorated and sparse. The bigger question though: how can I be a pie?

Tomato pies are a staple in Southern kitchens during the long, hot summers. The traditional pie is made from ripe tomatoes, cheddar cheese, and mayonnaise, thrown into a pie shell and baked until it is one gooey bite of goodness. I wanted to take this pie and update it. Make it a bit more modern but keep its traditional roots. Make the flavors pop with the barest of fresh ingredients. Make it easy for the busy mom and working wife. And somehow, make it reflect a bit of me.

To write my pieography, I start with traditional pie crust dough. If I have the luxury of time, I make my own flaky crust, but if it's been a harried day filled with family demands, I whip out a package of roll-out dough and make a free-form tart on a baking sheet. Within just a few minutes in a hot oven, the pastry is golden brown, and my blank page awaits. My first chapter must be about living in the South with gardens overflowing with fresh vegetables. So I layer local tomatoes from my farm share, bursting with flavor, to begin my story. If I'm feeling particularly sassy and can't find that perfect tomato, I'll use some sundried tomatoes marinated in a rich herb-infused oil.

The next chapter must be about Bermuda, so I need large sweet onions, slowly caramelized in my favorite Le Creuset skillet or cooked overnight to an amber glow in a slow cooker. I must tell about my love of things modern, so goat cheese combined with crisp bacon and meltingly sweet onions take the place of the traditional cheddar cheese and mayonnaise.

Finally, I add a flourish of basil chiffonade, part decoration to an otherwise unadorned pie, and part homage to my favorite thing about life as a cook: an unexpected bite of flavor.

41

Tomato & Caramelized Onion Pie

makes one 9-inch tart

2 ripe tomatoes, approximately 1 pound

Salt

1 9-inch tart shell or pie crust

1–2 medium onions, preferably Vidalias
   or other sweet onion

2–3 TB. olive oil

1 tsp. sugar

2 TB. red wine vinegar

1 cup goat cheese, crumbled, divided

2–3 TB. fresh basil chiffonade

3 slices cooked bacon, crumbled

1. Preheat oven to 400°F.

2. Slice tomatoes in ½-inch slices and lay on paper towel. Sprinkle with salt and let drain for 30 minutes. Flip tomatoes after 15 minutes and let drain on opposite side.

3. Pierce pie crust several times with fork. Crumple sheet of parchment paper. Open up, place over crust, and fill with pie weights or dried beans. Bake for 10–12 minutes or until golden. If using a store-bought frozen pie crust, follow package directions. Set aside to cool.

4. Reduce heat to 350°F.

5. Cut onions in half from stem to root. Place flat side down and slice in ½" slices.

6. Heat olive oil in large skillet. Add onions, sprinkle with salt, and cook slowly over low heat, stirring frequently, until onions begin to caramelize, about 8 minutes.

7. Stir in sugar and vinegar; cook until onions are deep golden brown, stirring often, about 15 minutes.

8. Sprinkle ½ cup of cheese over pie crust. Place tomatoes in an overlapping design over cheese layer. Sprinkle with basil, bacon, onions, and remaining cheese, to taste.

9. Bake 20–30 minutes or until tomatoes are tender. Serve hot or cold.

ANGELA J. REED

Angela J. Reed lives in the country suburbs of Chicago, Illinois. She freelances as a stylist, writer, and photographer in Chicago and the surrounding areas. She is also known as the lifestyle blogger "Parisienne Farmgirl" (ParisienneFarmgirl.com). On her blog, she uniquely combines the two worlds that fascinate her most—Parisian life and farm life—through journaling her designs, styling, and cooking. Angela was featured with her daughter on the cover of *Where Women Cook* in 2011.

In spring of 2012, she launched the subscription-based publication *Parisienne Farmgirl Magazine: Blending Country Life Simplicity with Champs-Élysées Sophistication*. She is also currently writing a Parisian macaron cookbook, *Makin' Macs with Parisienne Farmgirl*, available in the summer of 2012.

Drawing from her extended stays in Paris and inspired by her lineage of farmers' wives, she motivates others to combine organic, simple elements of a rural lifestyle with the elegance and glamour of city life.

You can visit Angela at www.parisiennefarmgirl.com, her magazine can be found at www.parisiennefarmgirlmagazine.com.

The heart of our home is beating with life. Children underfoot, breakfast dishes, homeschooling to begin, a husband waiting patiently for the French press to steep. My mind makes the switch from morning cleanup to the inevitable question: "What's for lunch?"

Swinging open a cupboard door, I blindly reach for a pie tin. I catch my reflection in its metallic surface. My "signature reds" and shock of brown hair are familiar, but a thought crosses my mind: *How would I define my life as seen in the reflection of a pie tin?* The cool tin begins to warm beneath my fingers as I ponder the ingredients of my life.

Peaches. Michigan peaches. I like them fresh from the state I was raised in, beautiful and jeweled with Great Lakes. I have four little peaches of my own, children so soft and sweet and easy to love. My pie needs something that gets better with time, like my husband. How about caramelized onions? And the crust would be God. Our God holds us together through miscarriage, job loss, and heart conditions, and cares even about everyday mornings like today.

Still missing from my pie is something wild and not-so-safe; there is nothing safe in the "for sale" sign in our front yard. We have a desperate desire to get this family on a farm as soon as possible. The unknown adds such a spice to our life. How about habanero-infused sugar? In my imagination, these ingredients combine in my pie tin and cover my reflection. In them are the woman behind the man, and the momma behind the children.

"What's for lunch, Mom?"

The question snaps me back to reality. I know there is crisp lettuce growing out in my potager, perfect for a side salad.

I put the tin down.

I have a pie to make.

Peach Luncheon Quiche with Caramelized Onions

makes one 10-inch tart pan

Habanero-Infused Sugar

 2–4 orange habanero peppers, sliced into ⅛-inch slices

 1 cup sugar or evaporated cane juice

1. Combine sliced peppers and sugar. Stir. Allow to sit overnight.

2. Sift before use, setting peppers aside.

Caramelized Onions

 4 large onions, sliced in thin rings

 3–4 TB. butter

 ¼ tsp. rosemary, crushed

1. Melt butter in skillet and sauté onions with rosemary until brown and sweet.

Habanero Crust

 4½ oz. butter

 4 TB. water

 1 TB. + 1 tsp. canola oil

 1 tsp. sea salt

 2 TB. infused sugar

 10 pieces of peppers removed from Habanero-Infused Sugar

 1¼ cups flour, heaping

1. Preheat oven to 400°F.

2. Combine butter, water, oil, salt, sugar, and peppers in small oven-safe bowl. Bake until melted and browning along edges of bowl, approximately 10–15 minutes. Remove from oven.

3. With slotted spoon, remove and discard peppers (use extreme caution with hot bowl) and quickly add flour, mixing with fork until you have a ball resembling Play Dough.

4. Quickly working with hot dough, press into tart pan (tart pan must have removable bottom, or pie pan may be used) using fingertips and heel of your hand. Press it all the way to edges and up along the sides. Prick multiple times with fork and bake for 10 minutes.

Pie Filling and Assembly

 5 eggs, beaten

 1 cup sour cream

 ½ cup flour

  Caramelized Onions

 2–2½ fresh peaches, skinned and cut in quarters (recipe works well with canned peaches thoroughly drained)

1. Reduce heat to 375°F.

2. Combine eggs, sour cream, and flour. Spread caramelized onions on pre-baked tart crust, and arrange peaches. Pour egg mixture over top and bake for 10 minutes before adding balsamic topping.

Balsamic Topping

 ¼ cup butter

 ½ cup habanero-infused sugar (without peppers)

 ½ cup flour

 1–2 TB. aged balsamic vinegar

1. Combine butter, sugar, and flour in food processor, pulse to combine, add 1 tablespoon balsamic vinegar, and pulse a few more times.

2. Open oven door, sprinkle over quiche. Bake for 25 more minutes (35 total).

3. Allow to cool and remove outer ring of tart pan.

4. To garnish, drizzle a few zigzags of balsamic vinegar. Serve with fresh baby greens.

47

SARAH BETH SMITH

Sarah Beth Smith is the artistic force behind Deeds & Petunia, a creative business offering everything from do-it-yourself tutorials and inspiring handmade crafts to event styling and multimedia art projects.

Known for having her fingers in as many creative pies as possible, Sarah follows her passion for art, craft, DIY, food, and laughter just about anywhere. She was recently offered the chance to contribute art direction to her very first stop-animation music video. Both challenging and rewarding, the one-day shoot featured neo-Victorian costumes, handcrafted hats, and candle-lit vignettes to create dramatic and authentic style. This year, Sarah joined the planning team for the 3rd Annual NW Vintage Wedding Fair in Seattle, a unique event offering authentic vintage items and local handmade goods and services to brides and grooms.

Sarah hails from the shores of Puget Sound in beautiful Tacoma, Washington. To see a glimpse of her world, visit Sarah's website at www.deedsandpetunia.com.

My pie is not conventionally beautiful or traditional. It's not what you'd expect. If you judge a pie by its cover (or crust rather) you'll see mine has a few scars and imperfections, some patched up bits and rough edges. But what you can't see is how delicate and rich that crust is, how it's been blitzed, kneaded, laid to rest, and brought to life again by experienced hands—until you take a bite.

My pie is savory, not sweet. Not your typical "American as apple pie" pie. My pie comes with a hint of a British accent. A bacon-y meat pie infused with dependable, earthy goodness—mushrooms, onions, butter, cream—staples in my kitchen. My pie isn't for everyone, and it certainly can't be considered light fare. But once you take a bite, you'll see how comforting and satisfying it can be. When you're curled up by the fire with a hearty glass of stout, sharing stories and laughter with loved ones, you'll find it fits right in. It tastes like an old family recipe passed down for generations. It tastes like the comforts of home.

My pie is the culmination of a lifetime's experience. My life began in the kitchen, with Mom teaching me a cook's most basic and necessary skills: the science of measuring ingredients, seasoning to taste, and trusting your senses. My learning continued as a young wife in a foreign country, inexperienced, and eagerly testing recipe after recipe on my darling husband, making mistakes and learning as I went. Today, I stand confidently in my own kitchen with a pie ready to bake and serve to my own family. Still not perfect, but perfectly seasoned, delicate, rich, and delicious—if I do say so myself.

49

Savory Bacon Mushroom Pie

makes one 9-inch pie

Pastry

3 TB. unsalted butter, chilled

¼ cup + 1 TB. shortening, chilled

1½ cups unbleached all-purpose flour

¼ tsp. salt

5–6 TB. water

Pie Filling and Assembly

10 strips of meaty, smoky bacon

1 medium onion, chopped

6 white mushrooms, roughly chopped

1 sm. pat butter

2 eggs

1 TB. heavy cream

Black pepper

¼ cup sharp English cheddar, shredded

Sprinkling of parsley, if desired

1 egg, whisked, if desired

1. Chill butter and shortening well. Blitz in food processor with flour and salt. Add water until dough starts to form.

2. Turn out and separate into two balls of dough. Chill dough in plastic wrap, in refrigerator, for at least 30 minutes.

3. Preheat oven to 400°F.

4. Cook bacon until crisp. Drain and chop. Save bits for garnish.

5. Cook onion, until translucent, in pan full of bacon-y goodness (*grease* seems like such an unsavory description). Add mushrooms, and small pat of butter, and cook for another 6 minutes or so. Let cool.

6. Roll out one ball of dough onto lightly floured surface or between sheets of plastic wrap. Lay inside 9" pie pan, leaving an overhang. Roll out other dough ball and set aside to top pie when you are ready.

7. In bowl, whisk together eggs, cream, and pepper. Add bacon and onion/mushroom mixture and stir to combine. Pour inside pie pan and sprinkle with cheddar and parsley, if desired.

8. Top with ready rolled crust. Cut off excess, and pinch to flute edges. Make a pretty design in center of your pie to vent. To be extra fancy, brush with a bit of whisked egg before baking.

9. Bake pie for 30 minutes, sprinkle with bacon bits, let cool before devouring.

TAMARA STOPINSKI

From a pottery studio design assistant to a full-time jewelry designer, Tamara Stopinski has been creating professionally for over twenty-five years. Her current work focuses strongly on the art of precious metal clay, to which she was first introduced in 1999. Tamara has since become certified in the medium and now shares her knowledge by teaching original jewelry design workshops. Her love for cooking is second to her passion for design and she enjoys farm to table, home-style cooking. Several of Tamara's original recipes have even been featured in area restaurants.

Nicknamed Talulah many years ago, she combined her nickname with her flair for fancy to create her business "Talulah's Fancy." The company launched Tamara's original line of women's jewelry designs and accessories in 2002.

In 2010, Tamara and her longtime friend expanded on the name to open "Talulah's Fancy and Friends," featuring her designs as well as those of other local American crafters. Tamara's work can also be found at select boutiques and galleries in the state of New York. For more information, visit www.tamarastopinski.com, www.talulahsfancy.com, and www.talulahsfancyandfriends.com.

My life & Fancy Egg Pie

My passion, next to creating in my studio, is cooking in my kitchen. Childhood summers spent on my grandparents farm is where I became truly inspired. It was there that I learned how to cook from scratch—often using what was on hand. Wanting to show my love by preparing a meal that is both memorable and delicious is also my inspiration. My grandparents taught me that working hard with true dedication to the simple ingredients of life can make your dreams come true.

My pie, like my life, is a balancing act of simple ingredients with a fancy flair. Like a traditional pie crust, my childhood was both rich with farm girl memories and the challenges of making do. This lead to a life rich in creativity that I feel both humbled by and proud of, just like my pie covered in a blanket of pastry and dressed with a pretty design or a guest's initials. A little fancy touch that represents my adult life filled with creativity, and the ability to achieve my dreams of designing a jewelry line and owning a unique, artisan retail store.

So my life in a pie recipe is simple—it's a fancy take on a basic recipe: The Italian pie I grew up making with basic ingredients like eggs, potatoes, and onions, and the flaky pastry that I began incorporating several years ago. My recipe now has smoky, thick bacon, fried crispy brown and salty delicious, because it represents my husband, Jimmy who loves bacon, who meeting and marrying was my dream come true, who adds flavor with his humor and inspires me daily! Utilizing the bacon drippings, I sauté the rest of the ingredients until everything lovingly cooks together. After that, scrambled eggs are added to the skillet until they are warm and fluffy. The pie is then topped with creamy cheddar cheese, blanketed by fancy, puffy pastry, and then baked until golden brown.

53

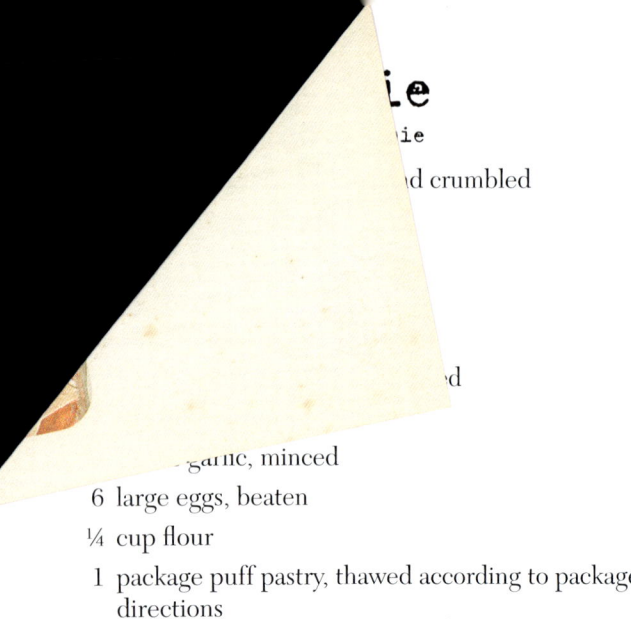

...ie

...ie

...d crumbled

...d

...garlic, minced

6 large eggs, beaten

¼ cup flour

1 package puff pastry, thawed according to package directions

8 oz. sharp cheddar cheese, shredded

¼ cup water

Salt and pepper, to taste

1. Preheat oven to 400°F.

2. In skillet, using reserved bacon drippings, sauté chopped onions over medium heat, until caramelized.

3. Add butter, potatoes, parsley, onion powder, garlic, and cook until potatoes are soft and browned.

4. Reduce heat to low and add eggs. Cook until eggs are fluffy.

5. Remove from stove top and lightly brown under broiler until eggs set up and any liquid is absorbed. Salt and pepper to taste.

6. Remove from broiler and set aside to cool.

7. Sprinkle flour on bottom of glass pie dish, and lay out one sheet of puff pastry.

8. Using large dinner plate cover skillet, invert skillet to remove egg pie. Slide pie into dish with puff pastry and cover with shredded cheese.

9. Top with second sheet of pastry. Gather sides of dough together by using drops of water, pressing together. Cut out initials from leftover pastry to top pie, if desired. Bake for 20–25 minutes until golden brown. Let cool, slice, and serve.

RONELLE van WYK

Ronelle van Wyk—writer, cook, and artist—calls herself a nomad. She says, "From childhood I always wanted to be somewhere else, someone else. I was born in a small goldmine town in South Africa. I met my sweet man at our university and together we've travelled the world, lived in different countries, and casually brought up two cute daughters while moving across continents. For ten years, we settled on the banks of the Loire in Touraine, France. That's a long time for two nomads. We got restless."

Now that Ronelle's two daughters have their own homes, she and her "sweet man" alternate between a chic city life in Paris and a muddy country life in Corréze. In her country life, Ronelle is restoring a 1800s farmhouse that rests near a forest filled with wildlife. She calls the farmhouse Coin Perdu, or "backwater" in English, and says even the mailman has trouble finding it.

In between her work and jaunts, Ronelle paints, writes, and concocts. You can read more about her country stories on: lecoinperdu.wordpress.com, about her food stories on: myfrenchkitchen.wordpress.com, and about her art on: africantapestry.wordpress.com.

Sitting by the kitchen table, I sip my morning coffee slowly, deliberately, and meander through my thoughts while staring out the window at the horses grazing the fields, lit up by the thin rays of an icy winter sun. My four Bantams are pecking their yogurt and seeds, and Ayiani is purring her satisfaction, content to reign the world from a warm lap. The kitchen table is chaotically strewn with writings and sketches of tarts and plates, recipes and ideas. A morning ritual is at play: warming up for a day of art in the studio.

Creation in the kitchen has much in common with creation in the studio. Though the tools may differ, the personal expression, the thoughts and preparation, the flaws and flops, the hunger for creating, and the desire for the process are all the same. The creative juices start to flow in the morning around the kitchen table, creating that recipe. Baking that recipe. Devouring that recipe.

"Like a bowl of fruit would give birth to a still life, this morning stirs my desire for a pie. It is cold. It is deep winter. My body asks for warmth, cuddle, and comfort. I start drawing and scribbling, and images rise of breaking through a crispy puff pastry to reveal delicate pink colored salmon, contrasted with plump white rice grains. Vibrant green layers of spinach, exhilarating whiffs of dill that weaken my knees. I succumb. Abruptly, the silence of early morning reflection disperses into a wild and cacophonic clatter of pans and bowls, spoons and whisks as I get bewitched by sensual flings of color, a pinch of traveling, scatterings of tradition, a touch of novelty, swirls of interpretation. A pie is born. I am here. Creating. This is me…today."

57

Salmon & Spinach Pie (Koulibiac)

makes one 9x5-inch loaf

1½ lb. fresh salmon fillet

1 lemon, juice and zest

2 small onions

2 TB. olive oil

1 cup white Arborio risotto rice

Salt to taste

2 cups water

1 TB. butter

2 large handfuls fresh young spinach leaves

2 large bunches fresh dill, finely chopped

10.5 oz. puff pastry

1 egg

Fresh green salad

Béchamel sauce

Pungent vinaigrette salad dressing

Optional

1 fennel bulb, finely sliced

Olive oil

Lemon juice

Balsamic vinegar

Salt and freshly cracked black pepper

1. Clean salmon fillet and poach for 10 minutes or until flaky, but not dry and colorless. Leave to cool. Flake, remove all skin and bones. Add lemon juice and zest. Season to taste and mix lightly.

2. Sauté onions in olive oil. Add Arborio rice, then salt, and water. Bring to boil, lower heat, and simmer for about 10–15 minutes or until rice is creamy. Stir in butter. Remove from heat and leave aside, covered, to cool.

3. Rinse and dry spinach leaves. Chop roughly.

4. Optional: Drizzle fennel bulb with olive oil, lemon juice, and balsamic vinegar. Sprinkle salt and cracked pepper. Roast for about 20 minutes until slightly caramelized. Chop roughly. Leave to cool.

5. Preheat oven to 410°F. Grease a 9" x 5" bread tin with butter.

6. Roll out half of puff pastry. Cut rectangle large enough to line bottom and sides of bread tin. Keep in refrigerator until needed.

7. Fill puff pastry base with some rice, cover with spinach leaves, chopped dill, caramelized fennel (optional), flaked salmon, caramelized fennel (optional), chopped dill again, some spinach leaves, and end with layer of rice.

8. Roll other half of puff pastry and cut rectangle a little bigger than top of bread pan. Place over rice topping and wet fingers to glue sides of top neatly together with pastry base. Roll out remaining pastry into desired shapes and decorate top as you wish. Brush top with egg and make a hole in top of pastry with baking paper to serve as a "chimney," to let heat and steam escape. Place in refrigerator for 1 hour.

9. Bake for about 40 minutes. Cover with sheet of baking paper or brown paper if top becomes too dark.

10. Serve with fresh green salad, béchamel sauce, and pungent vinaigrette.

Tip: Add a sprinkling of dried yellow/orange flower petals between the rice and spinach layer for a colorful version: zinnia petals, begonia, geraniums, marguerites, sunflowers, or nasturtiums.

Sweet

KATIE
CAMARRO

Katie Camarro—CEO of Greenfield's Greatest Food Company Inc., purveyors of Sundaes Best Hot Fudge Sauce—is celebrating ten years of sweetness. Prior to that, she owned her own marketing and consulting business.

Katie has been a guest on the Food Network's program *Roker on the Road* and a celebrity judge on *Throwdown with Bobby Flay*. She, her company, and her legendary hot fudge sauce have also been featured in the magazines *Everyday with Rachel Ray*, *Where Women Cook*, and *The Nibble Gourmet*. Greenfield's Greatest Food Company was recently highlighted on dailygrommet.com, an online marketplace that promotes innovative products and services to a large readership.

A Wells College graduate, Katie lives in Historic Saratoga Springs, New York, with her husband Jeff, and her two Great Pyrenees, Sundae and Esher.

Katie's philosophy on food is simple: "Life is short, eat dessert first!"

Visit Katie at www.sundaesbest.com.

As a proprietress, sweets chef, daughter, sister, auntie, wife, friend, and chocolate lover, those who know me will agree that my life as a pie would be a Chocolate Maple Walnut Hot Fudge Ice Cream Pie.

Simple, enthusiastic, sweet, happy, determined, nutty, funny, passionate, nontraditional, hard-working, loyal, and vintage-inspired. All of these words describe my life in the form of a pie that's baked in a well-worn tin with a shiny patina. My pie is nothing fancy: just the honest, real deal.

Serving up a chocolaty combination of crunch and cool, my pie has creamy layers with lots of personality, covered in fluffy wit and nutty bits. It's a near-perfect representation of my blessed life.

The chocolate graham cracker crust is a twist on the traditional—not too crazy but by no means ordinary. It mirrors the solid foundation in my life, with a family who encourages me to live my dreams.

The maple walnut ice cream reminds me of my grandparents and the grove of maple trees on the farm where I live. Ice cream serves as a source of sentimental comfort. It's always willing to please and comes in a variety of flavors. It rarely disappoints—a great mantra to build a life on.

The hot fudge carries the biggest reward. It's hardworking from bean to sauce, determinedly competitive, garnering attention with complex layers of flavor that make endorphins leap with passion.

The fluffy whipped cream represents loyalty and optimism—perpetually happy and aware of where it belongs. And finally, the nuts have all the fun. Like me, they love a party.

Chocolate Maple Walnut
Hot Fudge Ice Cream Pie

makes one 9-inch pie

Chocolate Graham Cracker Crust

> 4–6 TB. salted butter, melted
>
> 1½ cups chocolate graham crackers, crushed (approximately 10–12 whole crackers)
>
> 1 9-inch pie pan

1. Add melted butter to crushed graham crackers and mix together.

2. Press crumbs evenly over bottom and sides of pie pan. Let sit.

Ice Cream Filling

> 1 quart maple walnut ice cream

1. Allow ice cream to soften before spreading into graham cracker crust.

2. Cover with plastic and place in freezer for at least 60 minutes. Remove from freezer, remove cling wrap.

Pie Topping

> Good quality hot fudge sauce (I, of course, use Sundaes Best Hot Fudge Sauce)
>
> Wipping cream
>
> Walnuts, chopped
>
> Graham cracker crumbs
>
> Maraschino cherries

1. Warm jar for about 20 seconds in microwave. Caution, contents will be hot.

2. Drizzle warm hot fudge sauce liberally over pie.

3. Top pie with fresh whipped cream, and garnish with chopped walnuts, graham cracker crumbs, and maraschino cherries for color.

SARAH CHAMPIER

Passionate floral artisan, designer, and creator, Sarah Champier previously worked as the personal florist to HRH, the Prince of Wales and mother of two darling daughters, Laura and Lydia. Sarah's love of flowers has continually replenished and rejuvenated her "soul on life's journey."

Sarah trained at art school originally, studied graphics, and went on to study set and window dressing. As a freelance window dresser, she designed and constructed the props for many companies, including Laura Ashley. Later, after marriage and children, she moved to France to create and run a restaurant with her husband, a chef with whom she immersed her heart and soul in French country cuisine.

Not one to miss an adventure, three years later, Sarah had an opportunity to follow her dream of becoming a professional florist. On passing her diploma at Perhore college of Horticulture Sarah's reputation led her to being invited to become the personal florist to HRH The Prince of Wales . For the next 11 years she travelled the land between Palace and Castle creating displays for an extraordinary man and his family.

Sarah now holds flower and food demonstrations internationally and is currently writting as a coauthor of a book of recipes and floral memoirs, all the while working on her diploma in botanical illustration.

In her words life is never dull!!

"Where will all this lead" she asks? Who knows, but its bound to be an incredible journey.

Visit Sarah at www.tastebud.uk.com.

My life is an orchard, a beautiful cherry orchard nestled in the crook of a verdant pasture. In springtime, boughs are laden with blossoms startled against the bluest sky, the air full of floral fragrances.

I spent my childhood in this orchard, playing and imagining. Always with grass-stained knees. I knelt for endless afternoons picking violets and violas. I would make bouquets and daisy circlets while giggling with the girls. I recall how I would gaze down on the hens scratching and clucking to each other as they squabbled over fallen cherries. Their bronze eggs would be gathered later for dippy egg and soldiers.

Watching from my lichen-covered seat I would sit, swinging my legs slowly. But there would also be tumbling, bumps, and bruises, brushing myself down, wiping a cherry-smeared hand across the tears in my eyes, longing to be brave.

As a young girl, my friends and I would shriek with delight as blossoms fluttered down on our heads, nature's confetti. We would chatter about imaginary weddings and dream of kissing frogs while marrying our princes. How could I have known that these flowers, weddings, and even princes would become such an extraordinary part my life?

As I lay entwined in the cool flower-strewn grass, I gazed at the swallow-speckled sky, popping cherries into my mouth, the flavors awakening my senses. I watched jets and dreamed of far-off places, now explored. My life is so blessed with family, friends, flowers, and extraordinary memories.

If my life were a pie it could only be this: Cherry Meringue Pie with Wings—my own children's favorite! I take them to that same cherry orchard, where we share cherries and make more memories, comforted and soothed by that beautiful place.

"Sometimes our fate resembles a cherry tree in winter. Who would think that those branches would turn green again and blossom … but we hope it, we know it."
—Johann Wolfgang von Goethe

Cherry Meringue Pie

makes one 9-inch pie

Pastry

- 1 cup all-purpose flour
- ¼ cup hazelnuts, chopped and lightly toasted
- ⅛ tsp. salt
- ¼ cup superfine sugar
- 1 stick unsalted butter, cut into small cubes
- 1 large free-range egg yolk
- 2–3 TB. cold water
- Milk, or 1 egg, beaten

1. Mix flour, hazelnuts, salt, sugar, and butter together with tips of fingers until they resemble breadcrumbs.

2. Add egg yolk and 1–2 tablespoons of cold water. Mix until it comes together to form a dough. Wrap in plastic wrap and refrigerate for 20 minutes.

3. Preheat oven to 375°F.

4. Roll out pastry on floured surface and line metal spring form pan. Ensure you have plenty of pastry for leftover trimmings. Line pan with baking paper and fill with baking beans or rice. Roll out leftover pastry and make into 2 wing shapes—think eagles! Place on greased baking sheets, brush with beaten egg or milk. Place in oven with pie taking higher shelf. Bake for 15 minutes. Remove beans or rice and paper, and bake again for 10–12 minutes until golden. Remove wings when pale golden. Set both aside to cool.

Pie Filling

- 3½ lbs. fresh or frozen red cherries, pitted
- ½ cup superfine sugar
- 6 TB. arrowroot (or cornstarch)
- ½ lemon, juiced
- 5 egg yolks (save whites for meringue)
- 2 TB. butter

1. Put cherries and sugar into pan over low heat. When sugar has melted, increase heat, and cook for 10–15 minutes until cherries begin to break down.

2. Whizz cherry-sugar mixture in food processer. You should have about 3 cups of juice; top off with water if required.

3. In bowl, mix arrowroot or cornstarch with lemon juice and 1 tablespoon of water until it forms a paste.

4. Return cherry mixture to saucepan on medium heat. Add in arrowroot or cornstarch mixture, whisking constantly until really thick, about 3–4 minutes. Remove from heat and cool 10 minutes.

5. With a wooden spoon, beat in egg yolks and butter. Cool completely.

6. Spoon into cooled pastry shell and chill for 30 minutes.

Meringue

- 5 large free-range egg whites
- 1 cup superfine sugar
- 4 tsp. rose-flavored syrup

1. Take clean bowl and whisk egg whites until glossy.

2. Slowly whisk in sugar and rose syrup until forming shiny peaks.

3. Place meringue on top of filling, forming clouds.

4. Push wings into middle of pie so they protrude above meringue and gently wrap tin foil around tips to prevent burning.

5. Place in middle of oven and cook for 10–15 minutes until meringue is golden. Remove tin foil and serve immediately. Yum!

Optional Decoration

- Handful of violets and violas or any small edible flower petals

1. Place decorations on meringue

ANITA CHU

Anita Chu, also known as pastrygirl, is the creator of Dessert First (www.dessertfirstgirl.com), an award-winning blog dedicated to all things sweet. Anita was professionally trained in the pastry arts at Tante Marie's Cooking School in San Francisco. After graduating, Anita started Dessert First to combine her passions for pastry, writing, and photography. Her weekly posts document her adventures in the kitchen through vivid descriptions and mouth-watering photos, along with recipes. Dessert First was nominated for Best Baking and Dessert Blog in *Saveur*'s First Annual Best Food Blog Awards in 2010.

Anita's first cookbook, *Field Guide to Cookies*, was published in 2008 and her second cookbook, *Field Guide to Candy*, was published in 2009. Anita's books and blog have been profiled in the *New York Times*, *Sunset*, and the *Washington Post*, among other publications. She has contributed her writing and photography to several online and print publications, and also teaches pastry classes at Tante Marie's. Anita is currently working on launching a new food magazine with some other passionate food bloggers.

1.
2.
3.
4.

I love getting creative when I bake: to me there's no excitement in making the same old basics over and over again. I enjoy playing around with pastry classics and tweaking them to match my latest inspirations.

5.
6.
7.
8.

That's why my life as a pie wouldn't be just a regular old pie. It would combine my favorite pastry dough, my favorite fruit, and my favorite "unusual" ingredients: pâte brisée, strawberries, and lemon verbena.

9.
10.

The combination of ingredients reflects how I see myself: classic yet modern, sweet yet quirky, and just a little complicated!

11.
12.
13.
14.
15.
16.

I love travel and I love Paris. I first started baking because I wanted to learn how to make classic French pastry. That's why my preferred pie dough is a traditional pâte brisée. Although usually used for tarts in France, it's buttery and lusciously flaky enough to work as pie dough. Add on a lattice top that lets the filling show through, and you've got a pie that's simple and sophisticated—the way I like my life.

17.
18.
19.
20.
21.

Strawberries are the perfect fruit to me: they exemplify everything that is wonderful about summer. I naturally love being outdoors, especially on warm, blue-sky days. When I smell strawberries, I think of my ideal lazy weekends spent berry picking, swimming, and then enjoying a slice of pie in the fading glow of the setting sun.

22.
23.
24.
25.
26.
27.

To give the strawberry pie a little zing, I mix it with one of my most beloved cooking discoveries: lemon verbena. This plant gives off the most intoxicating lemony scent and the leaves impart an intense lemon flavor when used to infuse desserts. To me, lemon verbena tastes like sunshine and always puts me in a good mood. I'm always happiest in sunshine!

28.
29.
30.

When I make this pie, I taste sweetness that results from not conforming to the everyday, and instead, viewing life through my own offbeat lens. My life is that much richer and full from taking chances and exploring everything the world has to offer!

"I Heart Summer" Strawberry Lemon Verbena Pie

makes one 9-inch pie, or four 5-inch mini pies

Pâte Brisée (pie crust)

- 3 cups all-purpose flour
- 2 TB. sugar
- ¾ tsp. salt
- 1½ cups (12 oz.) unsalted butter, cold, cut into ½-inch pieces
- ½ cup water, very cold

1. Combine flour, sugar, and salt in a large mixing bowl.

2. Add about a third of butter into bowl. Keep remaining butter in refrigerator to keep cold. Use a pastry blender or two knives to cut butter into flour mixture until it resembles coarse crumbs.

3. Add another third of butter to bowl in same way, and then remaining butter. Do not overwork mixture.

4. Drizzle ice water over mixture and use fork to stir mixture until it just starts to clump together. Do not work it into one homogeneous ball of dough. Pieces of dough should just stick together when you press them together. Add a little more water if dough is still too dry and crumbly.

5. Form dough into two balls. Flatten into disks, wrap in plastic, and chill for 1 hour to firm.

6. Roll one disk of dough out into 13" circle. Fit into 9" pie pan and trim edges so there is about a ½" overhang. Or, you can cut out circles and fit them into mini pie pans—you can get about four 5" mini pies if you are careful. Chill pie crust while you make filling.

Pie Filling and Assembly

- 20 oz. strawberries, hulled and quartered
- ¼ cup brown sugar
- ¼ cup sugar
- 1½ TB. flour
- ¼ tsp. salt
- 16 lemon verbena leaves
- Turbinado sugar

1. For filling: combine strawberries, sugars, flour, salt, and verbena leaves together in a medium bowl.

2. Preheat oven to 350°F.

3. Take out pie crust and pour in filling.

4. Roll out second disk of dough to 13" circle. Using knife or pastry cutter, cut fourteen ½" strips of dough. Lay strips over pie filling in lattice pattern. Press ends of dough strips into bottom crust. Brush lattice lightly with water and sprinkle turbinado sugar over top.

5. Bake pie for 1 hour to 1 hour and 15 minutes, until crust is golden brown and fruit is bubbling (may take less time for mini pies). Let cool on wire rack before serving.

Julie Cove

With her natural passion for creative pursuits, Julie Cove knew she had to study design. That education has given her "the perfect set of tools" for a journey that has included interior design, retail, and, most recently photography, styling, and healthy recipe creation. Ultimately, Julie's goal is to inspire and energize people's lives with nutritious food that is delicious and beautiful. She hopes to set people on a journey to better health and a clearer understanding of how food affects their bodies. In her words, "I thank the universe for a health crisis that forced me to learn how alkalizing our bodies can reduce illness and disease."

Julie is deeply passionate about sharing a healthy, revitalizing lifestyle that prevents and helps to reverse disease, which is crucial in resolving the enormous health crises that many people face today. She shares her passion for healthy living on her blog while she begins a new chapter of her life: studying holistic nutrition. To learn more about Julie, please visit www.alkalinesisters.com.

My life & Raw Cranberry Pie

My life is like a jar of pie! *Hmm, really?* you might ask. Well, the closer I examine this recipe, the more I see that my pie reflects my journey of leading and sharing greater health with an alkaline lifestyle.

The fresh ingredients in this raw pie are full of life force, something I feel every day when I wake up, enjoying another day to share with others on how to live a full life. Having a passion you LOVE to share is incredibly beneficial to health, and my passion for healthy food invigorates me just like a serving of this pie!

The earthy sweet buckwheat crust is the foundation of my life. Influenced by my passion for design, it forms the basis of everything that I have done in my life. The pure vanilla brings out the flavor of the rest of the pie.

Raw cranberries and a fresh pear filling combine like the creative juices in my life. Sometimes I like to use purple figs and cardamom, or other times I use mango and lime zest. A variety of scrumptious creative combinations enlivens my tastebuds and my pie. The final layer is moist, yet crumbly, with nutrient-dense raw almonds and pecans sprinkled with allspice, sweet cinnamon, and zesty cloves!

The layers of this delicious portable pie-in-a-jar come together in every bite. The tart-yet-sweet raw cranberries offer a fresh new flavor combination that mirrors my new journey as a creative nutrition student and a healthy, alkaline food blogger.

Raw Cranberry Pie—To Go!

makes six 6-ounce servings

Pie Crust

   1 cup raw untoasted buckwheat, soaked
      (see directions)

   ¼ tsp. cinnamon

   ½ organic orange, juiced

   2 TB. maple syrup

   ½ tsp. vanilla

1. Soak buckwheat in filtered water for 20–30 minutes. Rinse and drain well, patting with paper towel.

2. In a bowl combine cinnamon, orange juice, maple syrup, and vanilla. Set aside.

Pie Filling

   2 cups raw, organic cranberries
      (save a few for garnishes)

   1 organic pear, not too soft

   ¼ wedge of organic orange, with skin

   6 dates

   1 tsp. cinnamon

   ⅛ tsp. allspice

   ⅛ tsp. ground cloves

   ½ tsp. vanilla

1. In food processor, place cranberries, pear, orange wedge with skin, dates, cinnamon, allspice, ground cloves, and vanilla.

2. Combine until well chopped and blended, almost a puree, but with some texture. Set aside. Rinse food processor.

Pie Topping

   ½ cup raw organic almonds

   ½ cup raw organic pecans

   2 dates

   ¼ tsp. cinnamon

1. Place almonds, pecans, dates, cinnamon in food processor, and combine until a crumbly meal forms.

Assembly

1. Fill jars with buckwheat mixture.

2. Layer with 2 scoops of cranberry mixture, top with nut crumbles, and garnish with a fresh cranberry.

3. Place lids on jar and tie a spoon to the side with butcher string.

Tip: This pie is ready for a picnic or a handy, healthy snack to go—ready when you are!

ALICE
CURRAH

Alice Currah is the award-winning food blogger and photographer behind SavorySweetLife.com—a family-centered recipe site featuring gorgeous step-by-step photos. With 750,000 page views monthly, Savory Sweet Life is a celebration of life, family, and good food. Featured by Saveur.com as one of their "Sites We Love," Savory Sweet Life is also a member of Martha's Circle (an exclusive network of blogs chosen by the editors of Martha Stewart Living Omnimedia).

In 2010, Alice was named "One of Eight of the Very Best Food Bloggers" by *Forbes*. That same year, she won Saveur's first cover photography contest. Alice writes a bi-weekly column for PBS Parents (*Kitchen Explorers*) and contributes regularly to The Pioneer Woman's Tasty Kitchen website. Alice's debut cookbook, *Savory Sweet Life: 100 Simply Delicious Recipes for Every Family Occasion* (William Morrow, June 2012), features a collection of family recipes, all photographed by her. She lives in Seattle with her husband, Rob, and their three children, Abigail, Mimi, and Eli.

My life has always been an eclectic mix of a little bit of everything with a unique, but identifiable, twist of "me." That is how I like to bake too, especially pies.

Although I appreciate traditional, classic, modern, and contemporary elements in just about everything, what brings me great joy is to piece all these things together to create something special and different without much fuss. Just like this decadent Kahlua Chocolate Pecan Pie.

Made with Kahlua coffee liqueur, this chocolate dessert is an outward reflection of who I am in this stage of my life. Before I started sharing my passion for food online, my life revolved solely around my children. Food writing provided an outward expression for my creativity, photography, and love of food, especially my love of really good pies.

I love when each delicious bite is an experience to be cherished, as opposed to just eating for the sake of having dessert. If I eat pie, it better be worth the calories!

This is how I live each day. If I'm going to stretch myself to be the best possible version of myself, every step of the way should be worth what I'm willing to sacrifice for it, without compromising integrity, and always being true to myself.

Consisting of multiple layers of flavors and textures, this pie is like me in so many ways. It's rich and deep on the inside, yet unsuspecting from the outside. It's sweet, but not over-the-top. And, it pairs well with a nice hot cup of coffee.

Everyday, my desire is to be a blessing and to serve others. Mixing the ingredients, filling the crust, baking the pie, and topping it off with a sweet cream is not just another dessert to enjoy. Instead, it is a ministry to bring a slice of joy to another, which is what I want my life to be all about.

Kahlua Chocolate Pecan Pie
makes one 9-inch pie

1 homemade pie crust (see page 146)
1 cup sugar
⅔ cup evaporated milk
⅓ cup Kahlua coffee liqueur
4 TB. unsweetened cocoa powder
3 large eggs yolks
2 TB. unsalted butter, melted
2 TB. corn starch
1 tsp. pure vanilla extract
¼ tsp. salt
½ cup semi-sweet chocolate chips
½ cup pecans, chopped
  Meringue topping

1. Preheat oven to 350°F.

2. Line ceramic tart pan with pie crust. Prick base of crust with a fork multiple times. Bake crust for 20 minutes until set but not browned.

3. In bowl, whisk sugar, evaporated milk, Kahlua, cocoa powder, egg yolks, butter, corn starch, vanilla extract, and salt until smooth.

4. Pour mixture into medium saucepan. Cook mixture on medium heat, stirring occasionally, until it thickens, approximately 5–8 minutes.

5. Sprinkle chocolate chips and pecans around base of pie crust. Pour filling into shell and set aside.

6. Make meringue topping and top chocolate pie with meringue.

7. Bake in oven for 10–12 minutes until peaks turn golden brown. Remove pie from oven and allow to cool completely, preferably refrigerated overnight before cutting into slices and serving.

Meringue Topping

3 egg whites
¼ tsp. cream of tartar
3 TB. sugar

1. Beat egg whites and cream of tartar using an electric hand mixer (or a stand mixer fitted with the whisk attachment) until soft peaks form.

2. Add sugar and continue beating until stiff peaks form, approximately 1–2 minutes.

Suzy Eaton

From a very young age, Suzy knew that she would become an artist. She's painted pictures, created murals, fashioned faux finishes for homes and businesses, and worked as a graphic artist. She's also written a book on decorative painting, but stumbled into her real love—styling—when she did some volunteer work for a Christmas charity.

Eventually, after becoming a freelance stylist, Suzy took food styling courses and attended culinary school in Los Angeles. She now styles both products and food for a large clientele. She continues to do set work for small film projects, such as commercials, and has been the set decorator for a motion picture.

Though passionate about her work, Suzy longs to travel more with her styling. In her words, "Traveling provides opportunities to learn more about local cultures and unique foods, which is perfect for a foodie like myself."

Suzy enjoys cooking and often experiments with new recipes. One day, she'd like to write a cookbook, to share some of the fun recipes and tips she's learned over the years.

How do you turn creativity, passion, loyalty, hard work, compassion, spirituality, and utter spontaneity … into the tasty ingredients needed to make a pie worthy of describing me and my ever-complicated, yet overly satisfying life? I guess I will have to break it down, piece by piece. The pie as a whole will be multifaceted, layers upon layers, complex … even discursive, as am I. A variety of elements that by themselves may seem semi-exciting, but together will compliment each other and make a complete and total work of art, subjective to its audience, leaving them to want more.

First, the crust must be stable, and support the whole pie. It must be the foundation and set the standard for the remaining layers to rest upon … but it must represent my passions and things I love. I love the beach and I love coconut … these things just happen to go together, so my crust will represent my tropical fantasies of lying on a warm, sandy beach.

The first layer, the main layer, will set the tone for the rest of the pie. It must be sturdy and strong, yet flexible … its flavor must work well with the other flavors. One of my favorite, indulgent things is, cheesecake … so I have no choice but to add the thick, rich flavor of sweet cream cheese baked golden, heavy and hearty…but wait, as nothing in my life is plain, I need to throw in something fortuitous. Little surprise mixed in… almonds, something a little rocky, but worth it … just as in life.

I have a soft, sweet side, and this next layer will represent that. It will be a combination of yet more luscious, gooey coconut mixed with my favorite thing in the whole world… okay, my favorite food thing. Chocolate! Dark chocolate, none of that wimpy milk stuff. I have a bit of a "almond joy" theme going on here. Definitely one of my favorite flavor combinations, fortunately I have more. We can't be done yet!

Éclairs? Another favorite treat. After all, I am so much more complex. Who doesn't love French vanilla crème? It's used in all sorts of desserts. It's versatile, a team player. It's smooth and classy, subtle and desired.

Any finished project must be adorned with accessories. Whether decorating a room or accessorizing an outfit, ornamentation is so important. I never leave without my accessories, so my pie will have plenty to adorn it. Did I leave anything out? There could be another layer, this is yet to be determined … leaving the pie somewhat unfinished, as my life … still to be worked on, improved on. The final layer? A mystery.

Tropical Chocolate Éclair Cheesecake Pie

makes one 9-inch pie

Pie Crust

- 1½ cups coconut
- 1 cup almond cookies, crushed
- 3 TB. butter, melted
- ⅓ cup sweetened condensed milk

1. Mix coconut, crushed cookies, butter, condensed milk, and press into bottom of spring form pan.

Cheesecake

- 4 8 oz. packages cream cheese, softened
- 1 cup sugar
- 1 tsp. clear vanilla
- 4 eggs
- ½ cup almonds, crushed (This is optional; it's great without them too.)

1. Preheat oven to 350°F.

2. In large bowl, mix cream cheese, sugar, and vanilla at medium speed until well blended.

3. Blend in eggs and mix well.

4. Add almonds, if you choose, and stir in.

5. Pour entire mixture over crust and bake about 45 minutes, or until knife comes out clean.

6. Allow cheesecake to cool about 20 minutes. Remove from pan and refrigerate until whole pie is ready to assemble.

7. While cheesecake is baking, make vanilla créme.

French Vanilla Crème

(It's acceptable to use instant vanilla pudding; just use less milk to make it a bit thicker.)

- 2 cups whole, 2%, or 1% milk
- 1 tsp. clear vanilla (using the clear vanilla keeps the bright yellow color, you can use the dark vanilla, but it will change the color of the crème.)
- 6 egg yolks
- ⅔ cup sugar
- ¼ cup cornstarch
- 1 TB. cold butter

1. In saucepan, heat milk and vanilla to boil over medium heat.

2. Immediately turn off heat and let sit for 15 minutes.

3. In separate bowl, whisk egg yolks and sugar until fluffy.

4. Add cornstarch and mix well until there are no lumps.

5. Take one quarter of warm milk and add to egg mixture to temper it, continue this process until mixed together.

6. Pour back into saucepan. Cook over medium heat, whisking constantly until thick.

7. Remove from heat, add butter, stir until mixed.

8. Cover mixture with plastic wrap and place in refrigerator until cool.

Top Layer and Decorations:

- 1 can coconut pecan frosting
- ½ cup semi-sweet chocolate chips, chopped
  Decorations, of your choice: chocolate sauce, candied almonds, small almond cookies, or chocolate cut-outs

1. Remove cheesecake from refrigerator. Place on a flat serving platter of your choice.

2. Mix together frosting and chocolate chips. Spread over top of cheese cake like a frosting.

3. Spoon dollop of French Vanilla Cremé on each slice of pie

4. Finally, decorate how you wish. Enjoy!

CARRIE FRANZEN

Carrie Franzen has been in the food industry for over twenty years. She received a degree in journalism at University of Wisconsin-Madison where she worked her way through school at Ovens of Brittany, learning baking, catering, and kitchen work. After that, she traveled in Europe for three years, specifically Germany, where she further pursued her love of baking. Carrie returned home and after various stints at catering companies and food businesses, she obtained a culinary certificate at Hennepin Technical College. While working as a school coordinator for Cooks of Crocus Hill, Carrie discovered her love for teaching.

Carrie has taught classes for ten years to various home chefs. She has also baked at several bakeries, including A Baker's Wife Pastry Shoppe. She has worked as a pastry cook at several restaurants, including Aquavit and 510 Restaurant. She is the former pastry chef for jP American Bistro, and for the last seven years, has taught at the prestigious Le Cordon Bleu. In 2010, Carrie received the L'Espirit d'Excellence award for excellence in culinary education.

1.
2.
3.
4.
5.
6.
7.
8.
9.
10.
11.
12.
13.
14.
15.
16.
17.
18.
19.
20.

If I were a pie what kind would I be? It's an easy question to answer: a blueberry pie.

My life is intertwined with this pie. When I was ten, I baked my first blueberry pie. My mother talked me through the directions. In her much-loved Betty Crocker cookbook, my faint girlish writing can still be seen. It's a pie filled with warm memories for me.

Blueberry pie is traditional, but never the same. The pie crust, a mix of shortening and butter for flakiness, resembles my tenderness. As a dessert, the pie is also versatile and flexible, as I strive to be. Whether topped with nutty streusel, dressed elegantly with woven pastry strips, or simply covered with a shawl of sparkly crust, blueberry pie always remains the same inside.

Blueberries, perfect in their simplicity, aren't always the obvious choice, like apple. But they are universally well liked, as I hope to be. The berry withstands a lot, resists getting old or moldy, and instead stays firm like a true blue friend. The fruit can be used simply, eaten in a moment of summer warm ripeness, or dressed up with exotic spices. Blueberries are also healthy, like me.

Blueberry-ginger pie best represents me—a traditional, down to earth, no frills dessert, like the blueberry itself. I like to keep it simple, with a bit of surprise zip in the crystallized ginger. The crust provides the foundation, keeping my pie's feet firmly on the ground, but on top are hearts of sparkly, sprinkled crust to represent all the joy in my life.

"Heart of Mine" Blueberry Ginger Pie

makes one 9-inch double crust pie

Flaky Pie Dough

- 3 cups unbleached all-purpose flour
- 3 TB. sugar
- ½ tsp. salt
- ½ tsp. baking powder
- 8 TB. cold unsalted butter, cut into ¼-inch cubes
- ½ cup cold shortening, cut into ½-inch cubes
- 8 TB. ice water

1. In large bowl combine flour, sugar, salt, and baking powder. Cut butter into flour until mixture is the size of peas. Add shortening; continue to blend until dough is texture of cornmeal.

2. Sprinkle half the ice water over mixture and toss with fork or fingers. Add more water, 1 tablespoon at a time, until dough can be gathered into rough ball.

3. Form into two disks. Flatten and wrap each disk in plastic. Chill until firm and cold.

Pie Filling and Assembly

- 8 cups (about 4 pints) fresh blueberries
- ½ cup sugar
- ¼ cup cornstarch
- 2 TB. crystallized ginger
- ¾ tsp. ground ginger
- 1 tsp. ground cinnamon
- 1 lemon, zested
- 1 TB. lemon juice
- 2 TB. unsalted butter, cut into small pieces
- 1 egg yolk
- 3 TB. heavy cream, divided
- Sugar to sprinkle

1. In small bowl, crush about ½ cup of berries.

2. Add sugar, cornstarch, crystallized ginger, ground ginger, cinnamon, lemon zest, and lemon juice.

3. In large bowl, put remaining blueberries. Add crushed blueberry mixture to berries. Fold in. Reserve.

4. On a lightly floured surface, roll out one disk of dough. Transfer to pie pan. Fold edge of dough over or under, and crimp as desired.

5. Roll out second disk. Transfer dough to parchment-lined baking sheet. Using heart-shaped cookie cutter, cut out hearts. Let hearts chill until needed.

6. Spoon mixture into pie shell. Mound berries in center. Dot with butter.

7. In small bow, prepare egg wash by mixing 1 tablespoon of cream with egg yolk. Remove hearts from refrigerator. Lightly brush rim of chilled pie shell with egg wash. Arrange reserved hearts in circular pattern on top of fruit (with sides touching), gently pressing over berries, until covered. Brush entire surface of rim and hearts with egg wash.

8. Chill until pie is solid.

9. Preheat oven to 400°F.

10. Brush with additional cream and sprinkle with sugar.

11. Place pie on parchment-lined sheet pan. Bake until crust is deep golden brown and juices are bubbling. Cover with foil if crust gets too brown. Transfer to rack to cool.

Quinn Hairston

With dreams of a handmade country life in the city, Quinn Hairston has started on a journey making and growing as much food as possible. Equipped with a bike-powered grain mill, four chickens, a worm bin, and patch of mossy grass, Quinn, with the reluctant help of her boyfriend, Ben, is learning how to cultivate, preserve, and forage for food. A self-taught baker and cook, she enjoys experimenting with ingredients and trying to recreate the flavors she tasted on her travels throughout Europe and Southeast Asia.

Quinn loves water, rusty metal, reading, and photography. She also enjoys learning craft skills and spends many hours making soap, binding books, and knitting. Though originally from the East Coast, Quinn moved to Washington state for college, fell in love with the gray skies of the Pacific Northwest, and now calls Seattle home. You can follow her urban-farm journey on her blog at www.Quinnwick.com.

Let me start by saying, I've never made this pie, but in my mind it's delicious. And when the day finally comes, it will be the best pie in the world. My life has been full of promises I made to myself—some unfulfilled, some done over a million times. I spent several years of my life, late childhood through my teens, and into early adulthood, dreaming of escape. Then, after I graduated from college, I spent several years of my life doing just that: escaping—or so I thought. Sometimes you start off with one idea, make a few mistakes, and what results is something better than you could have planned for.

I traveled and lived throughout Europe, and then later Southeast Asia. While I was away, I discovered all the pieces of myself that I didn't realize I had lost—each one by accident, or by making a "mistake." Now that I'm back in the U.S., I miss that carefree travel, but I have started on a brand-new, mistake-ridden life that has freed me to become more of myself than ever before.

I recently decided to become more handmade. I bought some chickens (the gateway drug to a handmade life) and a hand grain mill. I am grinding my way to a better me. The other week, I was making some apple pie cookies, and with the apple pieces I had left over, I made some simple apple jam. After boiling them down with some water, I added the sugar and tasted my creation. It was good, but I knew it could be better. I grabbed the powered ginger, intending to shake a bit in. If I'd bothered to look, I would have seen there were no holes for shaking, just a big opening. I poured half the jar of ginger into the apples and panicked. Then I gave it a stir and tasted it. It was AMAZING! I had to rename it ginger apple jam (since it now had more ginger than apples). I developed my accidental recipe into ginger apple cranberry sauce for Thanksgiving, but I believe this would make a great pie—ginger apple jam pie.

This pie, like life, can be amended depending on what you have on hand.

Ginger Apple Jam Pie

makes one 9-ich pie

Double Pie Crust

- 1¼ cups flour
- ¼ tsp. salt
- ⅓ cup cold butter
- 3–4 TB. ice-cold water

1. Combine flour and salt in mixing bowl.
2. With pastry cutter, cut in butter until mixture resembles coarse meal.
3. Add ice water, 1 tablespoon at a time, until mixture sticks together.
4. On a floured surface, roll pastry into two 12" circles. Place 1 pastry into pie pan.

Pie Filling and Assembly

- 4 lbs. apples (your favorite), peeled and cored
- ½ cup water
- 2 cups sugar
  - Cinnamon to taste
  - Nutmeg to taste
  - Ginger powder (Don't measure; just shake to the beat of the song in your head.)
  - A little lemon juice
  - Double pie crust

1. Preheat oven to 375°F.
2. Cut up apples and separate into two piles of 2 pounds each. Put 2 pounds into a pot with about ½ cup of water.
3. Bring apples to boil, then let them simmer until a very chunky sauce.
4. Stir in sugar, cinnamon, nutmeg, ginger, and lemon juice. Let simmer for a few minutes. Then taste and adjust any spices or sweetness.
5. Add remaining apples and let simmer for 3–5 minutes. Put filling into first pie crust and place second crust on top. Make slits in top of pie crust to let steam out while baking.
6. Bake for 50 minutes or until crust is golden brown.

VICKIE HUTCHINS & JO ANN MARTIN

Vickie Hutchins and Jo Ann Martin started out as next-door neighbors with a dream to find a way to feed their creative passions and still stay home with their young children. Through their early mail-order catalog, they found an immediate connection with customers and it wasn't long before they began receiving letters, photos, and recipes from these new friends. In 1992, they created their very first *Gooseberry Patch* cookbook compiled from hundreds of these recipes and the rest, as they say, is history.

Today, over 25 years later, they are still the best of friends and their *Gooseberry Patch* cookbooks are national bestsellers. With over 200 titles published, they are some of the most collected and cherished cookbooks on the market today. Each book is filled with home-style recipes from cooks across the country, and with each tasty dish, readers can read the story behind the recipe. This community of contributors and fans has grown into a passionate following. Vickie and Jo Ann feel fortunate to have made so many connections and shared so many stories over the years. They both reside in Ohio with their families and can be reached through their website, www.gooseberrypatch.com.

Starting with a foundation of made-from-scratch flavors, we both grew up with a love and appreciation of homemade meals and the magic that comes from the kitchen. And, even though we share this love and many others as friends, it's our differences that have made the partnership behind Gooseberry Patch work so well. We knew that if our lives were combined to make one pie, there would have to be not just one but two flavors that remained distinct in every bite.

Once we knew that much, one recipe immediately came to mind—a tried-and-true recipe from our dear friend Doris, called Dreamy Chocolate Pecan Pie. The combination of the rich chocolate chips (Vickie, the creative dreamer) and the nutty pecans (Jo Ann, the nuts-and-bolts business manager) gives the pie its signature flavor. Like these tastes, we work well together and complement each other.

While chocolate and pecans are the flavors you might notice first in our pie, it's the unseen ingredients—eggs, sugar, butter, and syrup—that are the real stars of the show. In this case, those ingredients would have to be the thousands of cookbook contributors who've been sharing recipes with us since the beginning. They may not be the first things you notice when you enjoy a slice, but without them, our pie wouldn't be much. In fact, our cookbooks simply wouldn't exist if it weren't for these generous contributors.

Ask any baker what their biggest challenge is and chances are, it's getting the crust just right: flaky and light, buttery, and crisp. The personalities and energy of our creative team create the perfect "crust" to support the inspiration and recipes ... this chemistry comes together to deliver something that all of our readers can enjoy!

Thanks to ALL of our ingredients for taking a little sweetness and a whole lotta nutty and turning it into a delicious reality.

Chocolate Pecan Pie

This recipe was generously shared with us by Doris Stegner and it appears in our cookbook, *Coming Home with Gooseberry Patch*.

Pie Crust

        1 cup all-purpose flour, sifted
        ½ tsp. salt
        ¼ cup + 2 TB. shortening
        2 TB. cold water

1. Combine flour and salt in medium bowl; cut in shortening until mixture resembles coarse meal.
2. Sprinkle water over mixture, 1 tablespoon at a time; mix with fork until dough comes together.
3. Using your hands, work dough into smooth ball. Roll out on floured surface; place in 9" pie plate.

Pie Filling and Topping

        3 eggs
        1 cup light corn syrup
        1 cup sugar
        2 TB. margarine, melted
        1 tsp. vanilla extract
        ⅛ tsp. salt
        1 cup pecan halves
        ½ cup semi-sweet chocolate chips

1. Preheat oven to 375°F.
2. Beat eggs slightly in medium bowl; blend in syrup, sugar, margarine, vanilla, and salt.
3. Stir in pecans and chocolate chips; pour into pie crust. Bake for 15 minutes; reduce oven to 350°F. Bake for an additional 25–30 minutes, until golden and puffed on top. Cool before serving.

CHRISTI JOHNSTONE

Christi Johnstone can often be found in the kitchen of her Arizona home, with her two daughters by her side, baking up sweets and treats for her website, Love from the Oven. Christi loves to bake, and shares her passion for baking with her readers. Love From The Oven features a wide variety of recipes that Christi breaks down with step-by-step photos and instructions, hoping to take some of the intimidation out of baking. Her recipes, photos, and approachable baking style have been a hit with both readers and major brands in the baking industry. Christi especially enjoys creating recipes that her readers can easily re-create, even if they are short on time and baking skills.

Christi has a master's degree in marriage and family therapy, and has a wide variety of professional experiences. She has worked in photo journalism, cultural exchange, marketing, design, and behavioral health. She now devotes her professional efforts to her website, www.lovefromtheoven.com.

My life & Brownie Pretzel Pie

My grandmother once told me that when raising children, the nights are long and the days are short. She added that the craziness and chaos passes by in the blink of an eye, and sometimes you have to find a way to slow down and enjoy the moments.

As I spend my days raising my two girls, I understand what my grandmother meant. I find that some days can be extra crazy and full of chaos. On those days, a simple yet special desert such as our Always Changing Brownie Pretzel Pie is the perfect way to bring everyone together, calm everyone down, and let us spend some quality time together. There is a magical moment when the sweet smell of chocolate is heavy in the air and everyone stops to breathe it in. I'm not sure if it's taking a moment to just breathe, or if it's the amazing power of chocolate, but a calm comes over the house, eyes brighten, and smiles work their way onto everyone's faces.

This recipe is always changing, as I often decide to make this pie at the last minute, realizing that the day just calls for it. With little advance planning, what goes into this pie is often based on whatever can be found in the pantry. If someone in the family has a particularly rough day, their favorite items may be what end up in the pie. The delicious combination of salty pretzels and sweet chocolate makes a wonderful base to this pie, allowing for creativity and flexibility every time it's made.

The combination of a pie, creativity, and flexibility go a long way in helping any mom find a way to slow down and enjoy the moments that will be gone in the blink of an eye.

Always Changing Brownie Pretzel Pie

makes one 10-inch pie

Pretzel Crust

    4 cups pretzels, crushed

1¼ cups butter, melted

  ½ cup sugar

Pie Filling

    1 cup unsalted butter

2¼ cups sugar

    4 large eggs

1¼ cup dark cocoa (it is fine to use regular cocoa in place of dark)

    1 tsp. salt

    1 tsp. baking powder

    1 TB. vanilla extract

1½ cups all-purpose flour

    2 cups of mix-in items of of your choice: semi-sweet chocolate chips, white chocolate chips, peanut butter chips, butterscotch chips, chopped walnuts, chopped pecans, crushed sandwich cookies, caramel bits, chopped candy bars, or dried fruit

1. Preheat oven to 350°F.

2. Crush pretzels in food processor. Once crushed, pour pretzels into bowl and add melted butter and sugar. Mix well. Press crust into 10" pie pan and set aside.

3. In in saucepan set on low heat, melt butter and add sugar, stir to combine. Heat until mixture is hot and well mixed, but not to point of bubbling.

4. While sugar is heating, crack eggs into separate bowl and beat well. Add cocoa, salt, baking powder, and vanilla with eggs and beat until smooth.

5. Add butter and sugar mixture to bowl and stir well to combine. Add flour and stir until combined. Add your mix-ins. If adding chocolate chips or candy bars, wait until your mixture has cooled slightly to stir these items in, to avoid melting.

6. Spoon brownie mixture into your prepared pretzel pie crust. Bake for 35–40 minutes, until set, remove from oven. This pie cuts and serves most easily when allowed to cool, but sometimes a hot piece of pie with a cool scoop of ice cream is the way to go! Enjoy.

Krys Kirkpatrick

As a girl, Krys Kirkpatrick learned to sew at "Gram's knee" which, she says, "has proven to be the best schooling I ever received." Krys's college days produced a two-year associate's degree, but she always excelled in sewing. In 1976, the women of Krys's family opened Elsa & Company, "a delight gift and children's retail shop" that gave Krys a creative outlet to grow her design skills, leading to the creation of her own company, Bunnies by the Bay.

Krys, along with her sister Suzanne and adopted sister Jeanne, are the creative force behind Bunnies by the Bay, which is celebrating 25 years of "glad dreams." Although the company originally created collectable bunnies, Krys and her sisters now design the softest, best-quality gifts, and security blankets for babies.

When she isn't conducting bunny business, Krys loves to draw and paint. In her spare time she travels around the country, showing her art with the band of artists that make up Earth Angels Toys. Krys has three grown children, a daughter-in-law, a grandchild, and her partner, David. She is one lucky bunny.

Visit Krys at www.kryskirkpatrickdesign.com.

My life & Creamy Carrot Pie

When I heard of this project, my first thoughts were: I need to create and draw a picture of my own unique pie. That instinct, in a nutshell, sums up what makes me tick. Carrot pie is a combination of my favorite pumpkin pie recipes with a twist. My life has taken a few twists of its own. Some would make you weep, and others would make you jump up and down with excitement. I'm hoping for the second reaction when you taste the creamy deliciousness of my carrot pie.

Why carrots instead of pumpkin? Because I am a bunny girl. (No, not that kind!)

The combination of cinnamon, nutmeg, and cloves are both familiar and comforting. They allow the taste buds to relax and savor the spicy custard. Each moment of my life is a constant reminder to slow down and take to heart the life lessons given to me. Practicing a mixture of gratitude, patience, and faith is as beautiful as mixing carrots, spices, and cream.

This pie has a sturdy and flavorful crust. My gram, mom, and aunties make up my solid foundation; they've encouraged me to be strong, independent, and creative. Those qualities are what led me, along with my sister, to form our 25-year-old company, Bunnies by the Bay. To this day, that group of loving women still encourage and support us.

Whether it's painting and drawing in my studio, designing the Easter window for FAO Schwarz, or sewing a soft, cuddly bunny buddy for a baby, I am a grateful and humbled artist who is blessed with the opportunity to wake up each morning and practice what I love. My life is the luscious bourbon topping and the crunchy candied pecans sprinkled on top. And, to quote my great aunt Ebbie, "Life is so much richer with a dollop of whipped cream."

Creamy Carrot Pie with Crunchy Graham Cracker Crust, Whipped Rum Cream, & Candied Pecans

makes one 9-inch pie

Graham Cracker Crust

- 1 cup graham cracker crumbs
- ¼ cup ground pecans
- ¼ stick of butter, melted
- ½ cup sugar

1. Preheat oven to 300°F.
2. Mix cracker crumbs, pecans, butter, and sugar. Pat into a spring form pan.
3. Bake for 8 minutes. Take out of oven and let cool.

Pie Filling

- 8 oz. whipped cream cheese
- 2 cups carrot puree, cooked
- ½ cup sugar
- ½ cup brown sugar
- ¼ stick of butter, melted
- 2 eggs, slightly whipped
- 2 tsp. cinnamon
- 1 tsp. ginger
- ½ tsp. cloves
- 1 tsp. vanilla
- 1 cup half and half
- ¼ tsp. salt

1. In mixer, blend cream cheese, carrots, and sugars untill blended. (You can also combine all ingredients in food processor.)
2. Add melted butter, slightly whipped eggs, cinnamon, ginger, cloves, vanilla, half and half, and salt. Blend until combined completely.

3. Pour into pan of cooled crust and bake for 50–60 minutes, or until a knife inserted comes out clean.

Note: I steamed carrots, then pureed them in a food processor. It takes about 3 bunches of carrots to make 2 cups of puree. A trick to keep the crust from getting soggy is to spread carrot puree on cookie sheet that has three layers of paper towels. Let sit for 10 minutes. This will absorb water from puree. Do this before you mix with the remaining ingredients.

Rum Whipped Cream Topping

- 1 cup cream, chilled
- 2 TB. sour cream
- 1 TB. rum
- 2 TB. brown sugar
- 1 tsp. vanilla
- Candied pecans

1. Put cream, sour cream, rum, brown sugar, and vanilla in bowl. Whip together.
2. Serve pie with a scoop of rum cream topping and a few candied pecans on top.

ELIZABETH MAXSON

Elizabeth Maxson is a creative entrepreneur who has walked, no, actually run, down many creative paths with great joy. Photographer, writer, editor, designer, store owner, and stylist are just a few of Elizabeth's creative adventures.

Her natural love of cooking has been satiated through writing and photographing for *Where Women Cook* magazine, and for the book *Where Women Cook: CELEBRATE!*(Lark, Fall 2011). She also worked as a contributing editor to *Vintage Vavoom* (Clarkson Potter, December 2007), and she recently photographed and styled her first book, *Quilts from the House of Tula Pink*(F & W Media, Spring 2012). Her work has appeared in the magazines *Where Women Create, Romantic Homes, Country Home, Elle Decor*, and others. She continues to write, style, and photograph for various publications, as well as for her blog, www.elizabethhousestyle.blogspot.com. Her work and professional services are available through her website, www.elizabethhouse.us.

Elizabeth is happiest when her creative work may inspire someone to achieve their own dream. She says, "The moment you stop saying 'if' and start saying 'when,' is the moment your dreams start becoming a reality."

It would be impossible for me to be just *one* pie. My creative entrepreneurial spirit has traveled many paths, and it would take many pies to describe them all. My pie would definitely have to be a pie that is up for adventure, which means it couldn't be so fussy that it requires refrigeration, decoration, or a prissy plate. My perfect pie needs to be portable, spontaneous, and sturdy enough for just about any challenge.

These little fried pies are like little savory stories that are told bite by bite. Who wouldn't smile when given a *whole pie* just for themselves? That is the beauty of a li'l fried pie. A whole pie, not just one slice, is offered and hopefully, accepted. That's how I see myself and how I hope others see me. I offer my whole spirit. Not just parts of me. The whole me. The sweet part of me, the burnt part, the flaky part, the soft part … all of me. Take me as I am.

My life is one surprising adventure after another. It doesn't bake slowly like those large, complicated pies. Instead, it continues to challenge me—moving from one frying pan to another. Sometimes, the heat of deadlines is what gets me popping, but it's life's variety that I cherish. Biting into a challenge is like biting into the middle of a fried pie; I don't know which life adventure is about to whet my creative appetite.

It's impossible to make only one fried pie. In my book, happiness is a pile of pies. Who better to share a pile of pies with than with my gal pals? My life wouldn't be complete without my gal pals…they love the *whole* me, burnt parts and all.

These southern pies are a tradition from my childhood. My father loved them and would buy dozens from a day-old bakery not far from our house for only ten cents each! I don't remember our freezer NOT having these pies. I loved eating them frozen, especially the pecan pies and the coconut cream pies. My mother was partial to the cherry-filled pies. They're wonderful warm, too, right out of the pan, and are still delicious when eaten a day or two later. And, of course, they may be frozen and eaten much later as well.

Li'l Fried Pies

makes twenty to twenty-five 5-inch pies

Dough

    4 cups flour

    2½ tsp. salt

    1 cup butter-flavored shortening

    1 cup + 2 TB. whole milk

    2½ cups vegetable oil for frying

1. Mix together flour and salt in large bowl with fork.

2. Cut shortening into flour mixture until it is quite crumbly.

3. Pour in milk and mix with fork until dough forms into a ball and can be handled for rolling.

Pie Fillings

Any thick filling will work in these pies. My favorite is coconut curd, readymade from the jar. So easy! Dickinson's Coconut Curd can be found in most large grocery stores, in the aisle with better preserves. Dickinson's Banana Curd is also a good bet. Add 1–2 small, thin slices of bananas to the filling. Lemon Curd is another favorite. These prepared curds are much better than store-bought pie filling. The jars are tiny, but you don't need much to fill each pie.

When filling pies, spoon round amount into pastry but stay well within edges to prevent from spilling out. Avoid runny fillings. The thicker and heavier the filling, the better.

Other fillings to consider: prepared chocolate pudding, prepared pumpkin pie filling, any fruit preserves, apple butter, vanilla curd.

The pies may also be filled with savory treats: meats, cheeses, mushrooms, and any leftovers.

Assembly

1. Heat oil to 375°–400°F in tall saucepan (this helps with splattering and keeps oil contained in a smaller surface instead of spreading in frying pan). Use candy thermometer to check temperature if necessary.

2. Tear off dough in equal pieces and cover with lightly damp paper towels.

3. Take one piece and roll out a circle about 5" in diameter. Find a bowl that is 5" across and once dough is rolled out, place bowl over it, and use sharp knife to cut around bowl to have a perfect circle.

4. Place filling slightly below center of circle, not too much. Fold over dough to form pie. Press down and seal shut with tines of a very cold, wet fork. Use a tiny cookie cutter to make a pretty imprint on top of pie to mark pie's filling with a design. For tiny crimping, use an olive fork, which has tiny tines. This not only looks prettier, but seals pie nicely. Keep fork in cup of ice water while working.

5. Make as many additional pies as recipe allows.

6. Place 1 pie on large, slotted metal spoon and gently place in hot oil. The hotter the oil, the quicker it will cook. Less time in oil makes a flakier and less greasy crust. Use wooden spatula to gently turn pie over in oil and slide it back onto slotted spoon to remove and place on paper towel to drain. Continue with remaining pies.

7. After pies cool, transfer it to fresh paper towel. Do not store pies in sealed container as this will make them soggy. If not eaten within a few days, store pies on a plate with wax paper. If freezing, place pies between wax paper and store in plastic bags.

Tip: These pies taste the best when eaten right away—very addicting! But they're also tasty reheated in the oven in the next day or two. Heat pies in 350°F oven for 5–7 minutes and they'll taste nearly as good as the day you made them.

MICHELE MUSKA

Michele Muska is a fiber artist who makes one-of-a-kind pieces of jewelry, quilts, and handbags sold at boutiques and museum shops throughout the US. Her work has been featured in many national craft and mixed media publications. Michele is also the PBS on-air talent for Simplicity Creative Group, where she also holds the position of marketing communications manager. This position takes her to tradeshows and events for the world of quilting, sewing, needle arts, and crafts. She is a board member of The Alliance for American Quilts, a nonprofit organization whose vision is to preserve the history and culture of quilting in the U.S. and internationally.

Previously, Michele worked as a therapist in geriatrics, where she shared her love of cooking to connect with her clients. She lives in Connecticut, where she enjoys gardening, making pie, and spending time with family and friends.

Visit Michele at www.lolarae.com.

My life & Midsummer Night's Dream Pie

I am a woman of contrast and surprises. So, it's only natural that this pie, with its unusual combination of fruits, would represent me. I have always gravitated to anything that is out of the ordinary, but I love to be steeped in tradition too, especially when it comes to food and my Czechoslovakian heritage.

The mysterious rhubarb plant, my pie's main ingredient, has many diverse qualities of its own. Its fruit is dependable and sturdy, tart and crisp, yet the leaves are large and poisonous.

You can always rely on me as a friend and confidant and I do love to party and be a bit naughty on occasion (although I'm getting a bit old for tartin' it up these days). But don't ever think about hurting my kids, because I might just chop up those leaves and put them in your salad.

I adore *Anne of Green Gables*, which is where the peaches come in, but my guilty pleasure is *Sons of Anarchy*. As the years go by, coupled with working in a corporate environment, I've conformed a bit. I would even say that most people think I'm quite nice. I can't figure out why they don't realize that I'm a *badass* on the inside.

Finally, I've included the beautiful and delicious raspberry! Like the ideas that continually stream in my ADD mind, if these berries are not used quickly they will be gone.

The lattice top crust is a must. If you are having a bad pastry day, it's much easier to fudge the strips than to roll out a full crust. And the little peep holes give you a glimpse into what's inside.

Midsummer Night's Dream Pie with Rhubarb, Peaches, & Raspberries

makes one 9-inch pie

Pie Crust

- 3 cups flour
- 1 tsp. salt
- 2 sticks butter, cut in small cubes
- ½ cup ice water

1. In food processor, combine flour and salt. Add butter to flour mixture. Pulse for 8–10 seconds until mixture forms a crumble.
2. Add ice water 1 tablespoon at a time just until dough clings together. Shape into disc, cover with plastic wrap, and refrigerate until ready to use.

Pie Filling and Assembly

- 2 eggs
- 1½ cups + few pinches sugar
- 2 TB. butter, cut into small pieces
- ⅛ tsp. nutmeg, grated
- 2½ cups rhubarb, chopped
- 1½ cups fresh raspberries
- 1½ cups peaches, thinly sliced
- 4 TB. flour
- 2 TB. milk

1. Preheat oven to 450°F.
2. Beat eggs, 1½ cups sugar, butter, and nutmeg with fork.
3. Place fruit in bowl, pour mixture over, and mix in flour.
4. Roll out pie dough and place in pie dish.
5. Place pie filling in pie shell and cover with lattice top.
6. Brush with milk and sprinkle with sugar.
7. Bake for 10 minutes, then turn down to 350°F for an additional 35–40 minutes, untill rhubarb feels tender.
8. Serve with cream or vanilla ice cream.

VANESSA BRANTLEY NEWTON

Vanessa Brantley Newton is a largely self-taught artist, though she took classes at both the Fashion Institute of Technology and the School of Visual Arts in fashion and children's book illustration. Vanessa is the illustrator of the Scholastic book series *Ruby and the Booker Boys* and Tori Spelling's debut picture book *Presenting ... Tallulah*. She wrote and illustrated *Let Freedom Sing* and *Don't Let Aunt Mabel Bless the Table*, both published by Blue Apple Books. Her forthcoming books include *Magic Trash*, from Charlesbridge, about the Heidelberg Project in Michigan, and a yet untitled collaboration with Bob Marley's daughter Cedella, from Chronicle Books.

Vanessa's illustration style is considered retro. Her artistic influences include American artist Mary Blair, and author and illustrator Ezra Jack Keats of the award-winning children's book *The Snowy Day*. When Vanessa isn't drawing, she's off somewhere singing, cooking, crafting, or writing.

Visit Vanessa at www.oohlaladesignstudio.blogspot.com or www.painted-words.com.

My life & Low Country Sweet Potato Pie

Rustic, buttery, sweet, fluffy, whipped into shape, and a little crunchy, around the edges would best describe my life's pie. It might not look so pretty, but it sure does taste good. My pie's rustic, because it's not easy being me. It's buttery, too, which makes for a rich, happy life. My pie is sweet, reflecting my good fortune to do what I love and share it with others, and the value I find in myself, the people around me, and my work. It's fluffy because the world can suck the life out of you and you have to be creative to find ways to fluff yourself up with encouraging and healing words. Finally, my pie is whipped into shape and a little crunchy, because, in life you have to work hard to get what you want and build up a crunchy edge to handle the tough stuff. In the end, my life and pie is still delicious any way you slice it!

For this pie, low country sweet potatoes are the very best. They ain't pretty, but the makeover is fabulous! I include lots of sweet country butter for richness and good old-fashioned vanilla. I'm a stone cold retro gal. I like the good old stuff! Oh, and forget about the calorie count here; throw it out the window!

That's how I am. I put richness and love into a life that's not always pretty, though I have the tools to make it fabulous. Richness comes when life and pie are shared, and not just with the folks I know, but the ones I hope to know. I serve my pie in a rustic cast iron skillet, which I then slice and place on sweet little hand-painted saucers. I'll serve it to you with all the Southern hospitably I possess.

Low Country Sweet Potato Pie

makes one 10-inch skillet pie

Graham Cracker Crust

makes one 10" crust (you'll have extra mixture)

- ⅔ cup butter
- ½ cup sugar
- 1¼ cups graham crackers, finely crushed (about 26 crackers)

1. Preheat oven to 375°F.

2. Melt butter in medium saucepan.

3. Stir in sugar. Add graham crackers.

4. Press mixture onto bottom and sides of pie pan to form a firm and even crust. For a crunchier crust, place pie into iron skillet. Bake in oven for 4–5 minutes. Let cool before filling.

Pie Filling and Assembly

- 4 medium-sized sweet potatoes
- 2 sticks sweet butter
- 3 cups sugar
- 4 eggs
- 2 tsp. vanilla
- 1 tsp. lemon juice
- Pinch of salt for taste
- As much cinnamon as you like
- Dash of nutmeg
- ½ can evaporated milk
- Whipping cream

1. Preheat oven to 350°F.

2. Cook sweat potatoes in boiling water. Peel while hot, slice butter over them.

3. Mash and beat with rotary beaters at high speed in deep bowl. When smooth, rinse beaters and continue beating at high speed, adding sugar gradually.

4. When sugar dissolves, add eggs, vanilla, lemon juice, salt, cinnamon, and nutmeg. Beat a few more minutes. Gently stir in milk.

5. Pour mixture into graham cracker crust. Bake until brown and firm in middle.

6. Serve with whipping cream.

Tip: Pick round sweet potatoes, which are less stringy.

JEN
O'CONNOR

Jen O'Connor's festive and artful persona abounds in her kitchen. She's an impromptu cook known to ignore recipes, making do with what's on hand; and, she's a relaxed host who always has room at her table for guests, and a pantry ready for spontaneous parties. A passionate decorator, she loves art, adores the handmade, and treasures the vintage.

Jen graduated as valedictorian of her class at NYU in 1991, and she then earned a master's in urban planning from NYU in 1993. She worked in small business economic development and the cultivation of urban markets, most notably in food and fashion, earning her AICP in 1995. As an expectant mother, she resigned her post as an executive director of a non-profit agency and began her own business, gathering and presenting folk art and handmade fineries, giving birth to her own business and first child in 2000. Now, she's mom to three little ones and the founder and owner of EarthAngelsToys.com, a retailer renowned for celebrating style and treasuring beauty.

My life & Iron Skillet Banana Pie

1. Don't even try to tell me it's a piece of cake. This is my life we are talking about. It's
2. pie! This is the tough stuff: my pie is clad in iron and ready in a flash, perfect for my
3. industrial-strength days as a mom and an entrepreneur.
4.
5. I bake my pie in an old iron skillet. I love old things, which is good, because I was raised
6. on hand-me-downs and junk shop finds. Learning how to like something for its raw
7. function—when it's what you've got to work with in cooking, decorating, or creating—
8. has opened my eyes to the beauty of form all around me. This helps me to see the best
9. in everything and appreciate the art that I find and sell.
10.
11. In my pie, I use brown and aging bananas that no one wants to eat, not this time because
12. I like old things, but because I never seem to find the time to eat the fruit when it's ripe.
13. Knowing how to use what's available and making it into something beautiful is a skill I
14. have long practiced. I pride myself on being industrious and self-sufficient. I'm sure to
15. add a lot of bittersweet chocolate chips too, because we all know that chocolate makes
16. everything better (and hey, all that dark chocolate gives me the antioxidants I need to
17. keep up the breakneck pace and juggle of kids, home, work, and life).
18.
19. Oh, and I must mention, I know this skillet pie tastes good, but I never eat it. I am
20. gluten-free. I'm used to doing things for others, and I truly never mind. I'm at my best
21. when I'm making others happy, whether entertaining, feeding, or sharing beauty with
22. them through my work.
23.
24. I bake this pie at least twice a week, because there is never enough of a beautiful thing
25. in my home. Besides, this pie comes from my pantry; it always seems full enough to be
26. a feast.
27.
28. Note: Some people march to a different drummer—I hear a whole different band, so
29. yes, this "pie" recipe will read much like a cake (you can now tell I am not a rule-
30. follower. I take risks and I'm a leader willing to live with the consequences of my
choices!). Trust me: you'll hear the music once you taste it.

Iron Skillet Banana Pie

makes two 10-inch skillet pies

2 sticks + 3 TB. butter, divided (I love Kerrygold Irish butter. Use the best quality you can find and stock up if it's on sale.)

3 cups flour

2 tsp. baking soda

2 tsp. baking powder

½ tsp. salt

3 super-ripe medium bananas

2 cups sugar

4 large eggs

1½ cups bittersweet chocolate chips

4 tsp. lemon juice

3 tsp. pure vanilla

1. Preheat oven to 350°F and place rack in center of oven.

2. Drop 1½ tablespoons of butter into 1 skillet and set in oven to melt as oven preheats. (Make sure it's hot and bubbly by the time you place mixed pie ingredients in your skillet.)

3. Mix flour, baking soda, baking powder, and salt in separate bowl, and set aside.

4. In stand mixer (mine is a cute green one) or with handheld blender, beat 2 sticks butter and bananas. Mixture will be lumpy and bumpy. That's okay. Life's like that sometimes.

5. Add sugar and beat until creamy. The batter will still have lumps. Relax, life isn't perfect.

6. Add eggs, one at a time, and beat. Add vanilla and lemon juic, beat until mix through.

7. Add chips. (Be sure to steal at least a few for yourself, but not all of them.)

8. Add dry ingredients and mix lightly. (Do not over mix, please. Enough is enough.)

9. Plop half of batter in center of 1 skillet. (Use a 10"–12" skillet and adjust cooking time as needed.)

10. Pop in oven and bake for about an hour, or until batter pulls back from edges of pan and fork comes out clean. Cool on wire rack and flip out of pan onto a pretty plate to serve.

11. Cover and store rest of batter for later, or bake second skillet pie.

12. Lick mixer blades, spatula, and put on water for tea to have with your skillet pie. See, that wasn't hard at all. You used what you had on hand and made something wonderful from it!

Tip: This recipe makes two batches so get yourself a second skillet, or make one batch, then the next. You may also save the batter for later, but don't split the ingredients. It's not as good.

JESSIE OLESON

Jessie Oleson is a writer, illustrator, gallery owner, and cake anthropologist who runs Cakespy, an award-winning dessert website. Her first book, *CakeSpy Presents Sweet Treats for a Sugar-Filled Life*, was released in Fall 2011. She writes a weekly column for Serious Eats, and contributes regularly to Taste of Home. She has also illustrated for various companies, including Microsoft, iPop, All-Mighty, and Taylored Expressions.

Jessie studied art at the Pratt Institute in Brooklyn, New York. She credits the artists of *The New Yorker* as influences—Saul Steinberg, William Steig, James Thurber—for their ability "to say so much with such simple lines."

In addition to opening a retail CakeSpy Shop in Seattle, a source for "the sweetest art and gifts around," Jessie is currently at work on her second book.

Visit Jessie at www.cakespy.com.

Pie, like life, is simultaneously simple and complex.

On the one hand, it is a simple pleasure, a nostalgic taste of sweet, carefree times. But on the other hand it can be quite complex—every small detail, from properly cutting in the cold butter, to the crust, to getting a just-right consistency on your filling, adds up to a greater whole.

Personally, I am a professional seeker of sweetness, but this is not to say that everything is all sugar all the time. Even dessert detectives have to pay taxes and deal with everyday life, but I strive to always remember and celebrate the sweet somethings that make life so much nicer (and to remind others of the same through my work). And so my life as a pie would have to embrace these contrasts, with an end result that would be lighthearted yet not lightweight, well-executed but not overly fussy, filled with a sense of whimsy but not too precious to be joyously and messily devoured.

And so, I present Cookie Dough Frisbee Pie, a real pie in the sky. I chose chocolate chip cookie dough to fill this pie because I couldn't imagine a more decadent or happy food, but technically, when it comes to the innards of this Frisbee pie, the sky's the limit. You can fill it with your favorite spicy apple mixture, almond-apricot cream, or even peanut butter and jelly. Why? Because this pie is designed around the experience. Baked in the shape of a disk, the ideal way to serve it is to lob it into the air so that it lands— and shatters spectacularly—on a pile of soft ice cream. The Frisbee Pie makes for a messy but memorable experience that is best enjoyed with a handful of friends. It is an opportunity, for just a few minutes, to embrace how ridiculous, wild, fleeting, and sweet life can be.

Of course, if this eating experience is too avant-garde for you, it tastes just as good served in fat, gooey slices, preferably à la mode.

Cookie Dough Frisbee Pie

makes one 10-inch pie

Pie Crust and Assembly

- 2 cups all-purpose flour
- 1 tsp. salt
- ½ cup shortening
- ½ cup butter, cold
- ½ cup water
- Egg wash (1 egg + 1 TB. water)

1. For crust, combine flour and salt in large bowl. Cut in shortening and butter until mixture resembles coarse crumbs.

2. Stir in water until mixture forms a ball. Divide dough in half and shape into balls. Wrap in plastic and refrigerate for 4 hours or overnight.

3. Preheat oven to 400°F.

4. Roll out one of the balls of dough to about 10" in diameter. Place on 15" pizza stone. On top of this, pat cookie dough into a circle, leaving about 1½" in diameter uncovered.

5. Brush part of egg wash around uncovered diameter.

6. Roll out second round of dough to about 10"; place this on top of cookie dough–topped round, and press down on sides, crimping edges with your fingers or a fork.

7. Poke top of dough several times with fork for ventilation. Brush with remaining egg wash.

8. Bake for 15–20 minutes, or until golden in middle and medium-brown on edges.

9. Serve with ice cream.

Chocolate Chip Cookie Dough Recipe (from Anne Marie Klaske)

- 1 cup brown sugar, packed
- ½ cup pure cane sugar
- ½ cup shortening, room temperature
- ½ cup butter, room temperature
- 2 eggs
- 1 tsp. vanilla
- 3 cups unbleached all-purpose flour
- 1 tsp. baking soda
- 1 tsp. salt
- 12 oz. chocolate chips

1. Beat both sugars, shortening, and butter until light and fluffy. Beat in eggs and vanilla.

2. In separate bowl, mix flour, baking soda, and salt. Add dry ingredients to butter mixture and mix until blended.

3. Stir in chocolate chips.

Note: Egg-free-dough may used in place of cookie dough.

REBECCA PELFREY

Rebecca Pelfrey is an organic farmer in Stillwater, Minnesota. As owner of Morning Glory Farm, she raises grass-fed lamb, Berkshire pork, organic laying hens, a few head of cattle, several hives of bees, and occasionally a dozen heritage turkeys. She became a farmer because she loves feeding people good food. And, she makes everything from scratch, including pie!

After ten years as an art director, she quit working to stay home and raise her children. The family moved to the farm when her oldest was starting kindergarten. Her second career as a farmer began slowly—a few chickens, a couple of horses, two sheep, and two pigs. It took seven years for the first milk cow to arrive.

Now, Morning Glory Farm raises thirty lambs and twenty Berkshire hogs a year, as well as maintaining a year-round breeding flock of thirty sheep, fifty laying hens, and a few head of cattle. Rebecca shares her farm experiences in a farmer/chef cooking class at the Cooks of Crocus Hill, where she discusses the meat her farm produces.

Life on the farm has given Rebecca, her husband, and three children a very clear understanding of where all of their food comes from. And, they have a true appreciation for the slowness of a good meal.

Visit her at www.morninggloryfarmess.tumblr.com.

1. Since I've come to live on a farm, I've learned to create more of our food "from scratch."
2. At first, homemade pie felt like a test; a good farm woman should not be intimidated by
3. mere pie. Pie baking became a personal challenge, and I set out on *The Year of the Pie*.
4.
5. The year started with a bucket of fresh-picked sour cherries. Three pies, made in quick
6. succession, got me over my initial fear of pastry. A tearing, unmanageable crust may look
7. unattractive as it goes into the oven on a hot summer's day, but the butter and flour still
8. conspire to delicious delight as they melt and flake in the oven. And, with a generous
9. dollop of fresh whipped cream, even someone who doesn't like cooked fruit can believe
10. in pastry.
11.
12. Next was an apple galette recipe from *Julia and Jacques Cooking at Home*—a labor of
13. love for my husband. This pie has a fabulous butter pastry filled with apples, currants,
14. dried apricots, and a brandy glaze. It's elegant and delicious. And I love that it is one
15. large crust, folded into a free-form shape. There is no pie plate to dictate the ratio of
16. pastry to cooked fruit, and the pie never looks under-filled.
17.
18. This galette pastry has become my standby. Sometimes it is filled with apples, pears,
19. peaches, or blueberries, and other times with goat cheese custard, caramelized onions,
20. and heirloom tomatoes. When I'm in a hurry, I don't even chill the pastry!

Rebecca's Favorite Pear Galette

makes one 15x12-inch galette, Adapted from Julia and Jacques Cooking at Home

Flaky Tart Dough

(always by hand, no food processor)

- 2 cups all-purpose organic flour
- ½ tsp. salt
- ½ tsp. sugar
- 1 TB. organic vegetable shortening, chilled
- 1¾ sticks organic butter, cut into small pieces and chilled in freezer
- ⅓ cup ice cold water, plus more if needed

1. Combine flour, salt, and sugar in large bowl. Using pastry cutter, cut in shortening first, then add butter and work until crumbly, with no bits larger than pea-sized.

2. Add water and mix with wooden spoon until just holding together, add a few more drops of water if necessary. Turn crumbly dough out onto large piece of plastic wrap. Pull up sides of plastic to shape dough into a rough circle. Fold plastic over and using heel of your hand, push dough out a bit to help it combine and to clean up edges.

3. Wrap tightly and refrigerate for an hour or so. I often just roll it immediately if I am short on time.

Glaze

- 1 cup apricot jam
- 2 TB. brandy

1. Heat jam in a small saucepan until bubbly, add brandy.

2. Let cool slightly.

Pie Filling and Assembly

- 5 to 6 medium, ripe organic pears
- ½ cup dried apricots, diced
- ½ tsp. cinnamon
- ½ tsp. nutmeg, divided, freshly grated
- ¼ cup sugar, plus more for sprinkling
- 2 TB. organic butter
- Whipping cream

1. Preheat oven to 400°F.

2. Peel, core, and slice the pears.

3. Stir in apricot pieces, cinnamon, ¼ tsp. nutmeg, and ¼ cup sugar.

4. Roll out tart dough until it is about 15" x 18".

5. Transfer to a baking sheet. (I use a small rimless baking sheet and then place the whole thing inside a jelly roll pan for baking to catch any extra juices.)

6. Brush center of pastry with thin layer of glaze.

7. Pour fruit into center of pastry and spread into thick, even layer.

8. Dot with butter. Fold pastry up around edges of fruit.

9. Bake for about 1 hour, or until nicely browned and bubbly.

10. Remove from oven and shake pan to loosen tart and keep it from sticking as it cools.

11. Brush with remaining glaze and sprinkle with sugar. Transfer to wooden pizza peel or cutting board for slicing and serving.

12. Serve with fresh whipped cream and a grating of nutmeg.

CAROLYN
ROBB

Born and raised in South Africa, Carolyn Robb is the youngest of five children. She studied languages in college, and then headed for Europe. After gaining her diploma in Cordon Bleu Cookery, she worked at Kensington Palace as chef to TRH, the Duke and Duchess of Gloucester for two years and then for TRH, the Prince and Princess of Wales for "eleven incredible years." Subsequently, Carolyn worked in Dubai for two years as a consultant and food critic. Needing to escape the intense heat of the desert, she returned to the UK and established her own company. Two years later, in 2005, she was married in California to a wonderful actor, only to be widowed shortly afterwards. After two years in the West Coast sunshine, Carolyn returned to the UK. She now lives in a beautiful corner of Oxfordshire with her gorgeous little daughter, a cockapoo, and two cats. She still cooks a LOT!

Carolyn is now working on a book with Sarah Champier, one that will be bursting with wonderful recipes and will give glimpses of the life behind the green baize door. She also travels abroad regularly with her new brand, "The Royal Touch"; she has visited Hong Kong, Tokyo, and the USA in the past few months. When at home she still cooks for and manages events for clients in the south of England.

Visit Carolyn at www.carolynrobb.com.

A Pie! A Pie! My kingdom for this Pie!
It's no ordinary "Steak & Guinness," Bramley Apple
or Lemon with Meringue piled high.
Mine is … Triple-choc
Zesty-orange
Merry-berry
Creamy-dreamy
Hint-of-mint
Schnapps (perhaps …)
Snowy playground on the top!
You'll want a bite. Then another …
Then it's hard to stop!

There's a pie in each of us that tells our own life's tale.
Mine's a little crazy, but that's me; spontaneous,
determined, obsessed by detail.
I'm a besotted Mum, devoted chef,
doting dog-owner and tri-athlete.

To cook is fun.
To ski … WHAT JOY!
Wind in my hair and snow under-feet!

I like perfection, nothing less. You'll find this in my
dark-choc-orange-pâte-sucrée crust.
It has deep rich color and a crisp light touch and
embraces a filling that's bright and robust.

I too am embraced, by my wonderful family;
Their caring love hugs me tight.
In one another's joys and successes
We always delight!

The filling is the life and soul within this unctuous pie;
Fresh-picked raspberries, white chocolate heaven …
"Oooohh" I hear you sigh!

A noble blend of my favorite things,
with stunning regal hues
With these I pay a happy tribute
and very fond "royal" dues
To my thirteen years at Kensington palace
—behind the green baize door;
Cooking for Charles, Di, Wills and Harry

(& sometimes even their special Granny!)

My life's been an ADVENTURE.
I've always loved to dream,
I'm driven to strive for goals,
sometimes quite extreme.
Through this pie I reminisce. . .
Who am I and where've I been?

The decoration on the top is styled with fun and flair!

It celebrates my greatest love; my gorgeous Lucy,
with ribbons in her hair …
Shards of chocolate, dark and white,
shaped just as you will
Vivacious mint, more berries red … Eat it up!
EVERY bit,
a-top a far-off hill!

Lucy is my sunshine; a sun that never sets
Her every smile reminds me, lest I should forget,

Those words of wisdom on my fridge,
that daily we glance

If you're going
to walk on thin
ice, you may as
well dance!

Triple Chocolate, Merry Berry, Snowy Top Pie!

makes one 8-inch pie

Chocolate Pâte Sucrée Crust

    2½ oz. caster sugar (or very fine granulated sugar)

    5 oz. sweet butter, cold and cut into small cubes

    ½ medium egg

    1 tsp. pure vanilla extract

    7 oz. all-purpose flour

    1 oz. unsweetened dark cocoa powder

    1 orange, zested (very finely grated)

    4 oz. good quality dark chocolate, melted

1. For the crust: Place sugar and butter into bowl of a food processor.

2. Process briefly to cream butter and sugar together.

3. Add egg, vanilla extract, and sift in flour and cocoa powder.

4. Add zested orange. In food processor, mix to point where pastry resembles coarse crumbs.

5. Turn into large bowl and bring together by hand, taking care not to overwork dough and toughen it.

6. Wrap dough in plastic wrap and leave in refrigerator for at least 30 minutes.

7. This dough is quite fragile to handle, so I roll it out between two sheets of baking parchment or plastic wrap, using a little flour sprinkled beneath and on top of dough.

8. Roll it to a thickness of approximately ¼" and line an 8" pie/flan ring or loose-bottomed pie tin. It should be at least 1½" deep.

9. Chill in refrigerator for 20 minutes before lining pastry with baking parchment and filling it with ceramic baking beans.

10. Preheat oven to 400°F.

11. Bake crust for 15–20 minutes.

12. Remove baking beans and return to oven at 380°F for an additional 5–10 minutes. Crust should be crisp and light brown.

13. Leave to cool.

Pie Filling

    1½ cups crème fraiche (I prefer not to use the low fat version!)

    2 cups whipping/heavy cream

    14 oz. good quality white chocolate, coarsely chopped (or you can use pistoles)

    1½ tsp. pure vanilla extract (not artificial vanilla flavoring!)

    ¼ cup thick Greek yogurt

    12 oz. raspberries (freshly picked are even better!)

    6 oz. fresh blueberries, washed and dried

    4 TB. Raspberry Eau-de-Vie (schnapps) or Cassis (blackcurrant liqueur)

1. Heat all of crème fraiche with ½ cup of cream.

2. Place white chocolate into bowl and pour hot crème fraiche and cream mixture over it.

3. Stir until chocolate dissolves.

4. Cool further before covering with plastic wrap and refrigerate for 2–3 hours, until it has thickened but is NOT set solid! (If it sets too hard it can be brought back by placing bowl in warm water and stirring thoroughly.)

5. Whisk remaining cream until thick but still flowing.

6. Fold cream carefully into chocolate mixture together with vanilla extract and Greek yogurt.

7. Return to refrigerator for at least an hour to firm up.

Pie Assembly

1. Spread 4 ounces of melted dark chocolate over base of crust and leave to set. (This chocolate prevents crust from going soggy!)
2. Remove crust from ring or tin and place on flat plate or board.
3. Spread one third of filling in base of tart.
4. Sprinkle all raspberries and blueberries on top of chocolate filling (apart from the 16 of each kept aside for decoration).
5. Sprinkle liqueur over berries.
6. Spread remaining chocolate filling on top berries, shaping it into dome.

Decorations

24	milk or dark chocolate sticks, at least 4-inches long
1	oz. dark chocolate, melted
	A little very fine red ribbon, twine, or thread
	A tiny snowman, skiing doll, or other figure to sit on the swing, maximum of 1-inch high
16	perfect raspberries (taken from the 12 oz. raspberries)
16	dark and white striped chocolate sticks, approximately 3-inches long (available from most specialty cake decorating stores)
16	perfect blueberries (taken from the 6 oz. blueberries)
16	white chocolate sticks, approximately 3-inches long
16	sprigs fresh mint
2	TB. white chocolate, coarsely grated
	Confectioner's sugar for decoration

1. Make the "swing."
2. Break 5 dark chocolate sticks into 3½" lengths.
3. Place 4 of them in center of tart, leaning against one another (as per picture). Stick them together at top using a little melted chocolate.
4. To make "seat," break another chocolate stick into 3 times 1" lengths. Stick those together using a little more melted chocolate.
5. Using red thread, twine, or ribbon, attach swing to remaining 3" length of chocolate stick.
6. Lay this across top of the two uprights and "stick" into position using little blobs of melted chocolate.
7. Position your snowman or other figure on seat of the swing.
8. Place 16 raspberries around edge at equal intervals.
9. Stick in striped chocolate sticks just to left of each raspberry, pointing out from tart.
10. Place one blueberry just above each raspberry.
11. Position dark and white chocolate sticks between blueberries, angled in opposite directions.
12. Place a sprig of mint between each raspberry.
13. Sprinkle grated white chocolate around swing in center of the tart.
14. Keep well chilled until serving.
15. Just before serving, dust with "snow"—a little confectioner's sugar!

134

Tip: For the curst, I double the recipe so that I can use the whole egg. The extra dough can be made into a second pie crust or some tiny cookies. Just add a handful of white chocolate drops!

MONIKA ROE

Monika Roe is an illustrator with an award-winning background as an art director for ad agencies in Los Angeles and Indianapolis. As an illustrator, some of the many clients she has enjoyed working with include: Disney, American Girl, Hallmark, Coca Cola, Absolut Vodka, Pantene, Coty, Avon, Rockport, the U.S. Postal Service, Toyota, Pfizer, and Microsoft. Monika has also illustrated countless book covers and magazine editorials for publishers across the country and internationally.

Her passion for cooking led to adding food illustration to her portfolio last year which has already attracted the attention of editors across the country. Monika's studio is located in the beautiful wine country of Paso Robles, California. Some of her influences are her world travels, Danish design, and the glamour of old Hollywood. You can see her work at www.monikaroe.com and www.illopro.blogspot.com.

1.   My Sparkly Pie and I.

When you see a pie with a buttery crust, filled with layers of deep, rich chocolate; creamy rum-flavored custard; fresh red raspberries; and finally, piled impossibly high with sparkling coffee meringue, think of me because that pie is me and I am that pie.

Let's be honest; I am the pie that makes a big ol' mess in the kitchen! I am the pie that doesn't think twice about using too many bowls, spoons, measuring devices, pots and pans because I will do anything necessary to reach my fabulous potential. When you lick the last bits of chocolate or custard out of the bowl, you can't help but savor life and taste what I'm talking about.

I'm talking about the ease of premade pie crust that demonstrates I've learned to be good to myself and not make things harder than they need to be. I'm talking about the dark, velvety sweetness of a chocolate layer that reminds me to live in the moment, because when I'm tasting it, it's impossible to let my mind wander.

If my mind does wander, it wanders to the next layer of lush custard touched with a hint of rum. It's a classic with a twist, just like my good manners that inevitably give way to my sarcastic humor. They say that's how we redheads are, unpredictable. Maybe that's why I insist on hiding a layer of red raspberries underneath the meringue. And the meringue! Oh the meringue!

My meringue is like my collection of high heels; it has to be sky high! You'll see my pie and me from a mile away, walking hand in hand and towering over everyone. Stilettos and soaring meringue make me happy! You know what else makes me happy? Coffee. So I flavor my meringue with coffee and then top it with edible glitter, sending it into a state of sparkling bliss, as sparkly as the vintage jewelry I'm known to wear.

Such is my life as a pie: multilayered, messy during the creative process, surprising, sweet, and no matter what, always sparkling.

Redhead's Sky High Stiletto Pie

makes one 9-inch pie

Pie Filling and Assembly

- 1 premade pie crust for a 9-inch pie
- 2 TB. water
- 2½ TB. rum
- 1 envelope unflavored gelatin
- ⅔ cup sugar
- 1 TB. cornstarch
- 2 cups milk
- 4 egg yolks
- 1 cup semi-sweet chocolate chips
- 1 cup heavy whipping cream
- 2 TB. powdered sugar
- 12 oz. fresh raspberries

1. Prepare pie crust as directed on package and cool.

2. Stir water and rum together in small bowl. Sprinkle in gelatin. Stir and set aside.

3. To make custard, combine sugar and cornstarch in heavy saucepan and gradually whisk in milk and egg yolks. Bring to boil over medium heat, whisking entire time. When mixture comes to a boil, cook for another minute. Remove from heat and whisk in gelatin mixture until thoroughly combined.

4. Pour 1 cup of custard from saucepan into bowl and stir in chocolate chips until smooth. Pour chocolate custard into prepared crust, and chill until set, about 20 minutes. Let remaining custard cool.

5. Using a mixer, beat whipping cream at high speed and gradually add powdered sugar. Beat until soft peaks form. Fold whipped cream into reserved custard and pour over chocolate custard. Smooth top with a spatula. Chill pie until set, about 2 hours.

6. Arrange raspberries in a layer covering top of pie, refrigerate while making meringue.

Coffee Meringue

- ½ tsp. water
- ½ tsp. instant coffee
- 6 egg whites, room temperature
- ¾ cup superfine sugar

For Decoration

Edible cake-decorating glitter in gold

1. Put oven rack in lower middle position and preheat oven to 450°F.

2. Combine water and instant coffee in a small bowl, stir until coffee is completely dissolved, set aside.

3. Add 1" of water to large saucepan and bring to boil. (Use saucepan that bowl of stand mixer will fit into.) Reduce to a simmer.

4. Whisk egg whites and sugar together in mixer bowl until sugar has dissolved.

5. Place mixer bowl over simmering water and stir continuously with silicone spatula. Scrape down sides of bowl and keep stirring until mixture's temperature reads 160°F on a candy thermometer, about 6 minutes. Remove from heat immediately. Be careful not to overcook.

6. Place mixer bowl on mixer stand, add coffee, and whisk meringue until it has cooled and forms stiff peaks with a glossy surface.

7. Pile meringue onto pie, smoothing and spreading using a swirling motion. Be careful not to displace raspberries. Make sure meringue touches the edge of pie crust all the way around. Bake for approximately 4 minutes until meringue is lightly browned. Remove from oven and sprinkle with edible glitter.

138

Celeste

Shaw

Celeste is a Spokane, Washington, businesswoman, entrepreneur, and contributing writer for several magazines. Her highly successful restaurant CHAPS opened in 2006 to immediate critical acclaim, garnering the region's "Top Table Award" in only its second year of operation. CHAPS annually receives acknowledgment from the food industry and voting patrons as "Best" in breakfast and family restaurant categories.

Not simply content with the success of CHAPS, Celeste expanded it, adding her bakery called Cake to complement the restaurant. CHAPS is now considered a "must-visit" destination for the area, as underscored and featured on the Food Network's "Diners Drive-inns and Dives" in November 2010. Celeste also opened a boutique shop PINK—a salvage, architectural, antique shop with dear friends in Spokane, Washington. Ralph Lauren, Eddie Bauer, and Nordstrom are just a few of the many shoppers who frequent the eclectic store.

Celeste's architectural, artistic, culinary, and decorating talents are not only on display at CHAPS, but have been featured nationally in several publications and books. To learn more about Celeste, visit www.chapsgirl.com and www.pinksalvagegallery.com.

Hello Pie! Lemon garnished, fig tart with rhubarb-blackberry filling, and cinnamon crumble topping. There is timelessness within your delectable design. You reflect the story of me. Therefore, I insist you be a little vintage, decadent, delicate, and versatile yet, unmethodical and unpretentious. I cannot exclude daring, however I am always amicable to modify—fearing no limitations or boundaries. This lends itself to my choice for wild blackberries and rhubarb. Fruits that are tart yet can vary to sweet. Ill add figs, a fragile and delicate fruit, to lend a sublime charisma. In unison with fresh, soft, snowy white tapioca pearls and tangy lemon zest, the harmony of the fruit, and a sprinkle of cinnamon crumble adds an unexpected surprise.

Its undeniably charming and delicious when taste marries quintessence. So my butter crust will be from a tried-and-true scratch recipe. The blending of intensity, texture, and flavor must be symbiotic and distinctive. I have true affection for the transparency of unrefined moments, and I crave an inspired life. I daydream about it imagining the true joy in every moment of its creation. I am unafraid to indulge. So of course only real, simple and unprocessed ingredients will do, pure butter, fresh fruits, and hardy spice, a reflective tribute to a sweet farm memory.

As in my life, like any dreamer, I want to redefine traditional and uncomplicated. Still I admire classic simplicity, recognizing that with a bit of added sugar and butter, it transcends into undeniable delight. So I choose fruit that in all its lush ripeness reminds me of my reverence for life. The flavors mingle together a classic simplicity, but offer a sample of Mother Nature showing off. This is my tribute of love to my farm and the earth. I use a fragrant Saigon cinnamon that gives the topping a very warm and spicy flavor resonating like a lingering kiss. My ingredients like my family, is a diverse mélange that individually is enjoyable but collectively is celebrated.

The comfort of traditional and memorable flavors is eclipsed only by the elegant and whimsical presentation, a little souvenir from me to you. Upon a vintage plate reflecting the glamour of old, a pint-size Mason jar reveals a tiffany blue ribbon and a label that proclaims "hello pie." A tarnished silver fork and a retired embroidered napkin are just right.

141

Lemon Tapioca Fig Tart with Rhubarb, Blackberry Filling, & Cinnamon Crumble Topping

makes four 8-ounce jars

Butter Crust

    2½ cups all-purpose flour
    1 tsp. salt
    1 tsp. granulated sugar
    1 cup unsalted butter, cut into ½-inch cubes
    ¾ cup ice water

1. Combine flour, salt, sugar, and mix well.

2. Add butter and mix gently with a fork or by hand.

3. Slowly add ice water, 1 tablespoon at a time, until mixture forms small pea-size crumbs.

4. Separate dough into two patty shapes and wrap with plastic wrap. Chill the dough for at least 1 hour.

5. When ready to use, let dough sit at room temperature for 10 minutes. Lightly flour surface and roll out dough to ¼" thickness.

Crumb Topping

    ½ cup + 3 TB. all-purpose flour
    1 tsp. salt
    ½ cup brown sugar, firmly packed
    3 TB. granulated sugar
    1 TB. Saigon cinnamon
    ½ cup butter, cut into cubes
    ¼ cup rolled oats

1. Combine flour, salt, brown sugar, granulated sugar, and cinnamon.

2. Add butter and mix thoroughly with fork until texture forms small pea-shaped consistency. Add rolled oats to create a crumble mixture.

3. Sprinkle crumb mixture over pie filling before baking.

Pie Filling and Assembly

    1 cup dried figs
    3½ cups untrimmed rhubarb, in ½-inch thick slices
    2½ cups blackberries
    ½ cup granulated sugar
    ¼ cup light brown sugar
    1 TB. lemon juice
    ¼ tsp. salt
    ¼ cup quick-cooking tapioca
    2 TB. unsalted butter, cut into small pieces
       Whipped cream for topping
    1 TB. lemon zest

1. Preheat oven to 400°F.

2. In small bowl, reconstitute dry figs by placing them in 2 cups of boiling water for 15 minutes and drain.

3. Stir together rhubarb, blackberries, sugars, lemon, salt, and tapioca in large bowl. Combine figs with berry mixture.

4. Mound filling inside bottom pie crust and dot with bits of unsalted butter. Top with crumble. Bake for 20 minutes until golden brown. Top with whipped cream and lemon zest.

ROBIN SHEA

80% Healthy, 20% Indulgent, 100% Southern

Robin Shea, "America's Favorite Sister in the South," is the new face of food and fitness for Southerners everywhere. Her Southern Fried Fitness Lifestyle program (television and radio) promotes living 80% Healthy, 20% Indulgent and 100% SOUTHERN; the result is a winning recipe for long-term, sustainable health and fitness.

Robin was born in Merryville, Louisiana, and raised in Dallas, Texas. A fourth-generation culinary entrepreneur, Robin inherited her love of food and entertaining from the masters she grew up admiring.

Robin lives in Bowling Green, Kentucky, with her husband of twenty-four years, Greg, and their four sons Colton, Mac, Rylan, and Rowdy.

Blue eyes and freckles 'neath a white cowboy hat
His two bestest friends are his dog and his cat…

I am a frazzled, busy, Southern mom of four boys. Complicated recipes and fussy ingredients are the last thing my pie needs. My pie must remind me to stop, breathe, and savor life! There was a time when life was uncomplicated, buttery smooth, and carefree, and that is what my pie will be.

My pie is a lot like my nanny's feather bed: buttermilk blankets softly beckoning the laughter of cousins. Ten more minutes PLEAZE … is the white chocolate gently folded into the creamy buttermilk for that little extra something special. The warm raspberry sauce is the last little giggle heard before tiny bodies snuggle in and little eyes get heavy. After hours of stories, laughter, and whispers, yawns fill the air and little voices give way to slumber.

My pie is a Southern pie. Being Southern is the essence of my spirit: an unspoken pride in having good manners, being kind, resilient, tough, and soft, all at the same time. My pie isn't hoity-toity. It's more like snuggling into nanny's warm bed with a crisp pillow.

Each of my childhood memories is flavorfully intertwined with celebration and Southern dishes. Baking and serving my pie is similarly steeped in tradition. From the familiarity of my nanny's heirloom mixing bowls to the curve of my fork, every detail enhances the experience.

My life is a beautiful blending of boys, dirt, dogs, horses, laundry, dishes, and homework, but my pie echoes my nanny's gentle reminders to savor my chaos!

Blue eyes and freckles and holes in his jeans.
Out in the back yard ridin' his dreams.
He's our little cowboy until the day,
The fences can't hold him and he'll ride away.
—Chris LeDoux

White Chocolate Buttermilk Pie with Warm Raspberry Sauce

makes one 9-inch pie

Pastry for Single-Crust

- 1¼ cups all-purpose, unbleached flour (a bit more for dusting surface)
- ¼ tsp. salt
- ⅓ cup butter, cut into small cubes
- 3–4 TB. ice-cold water

1. In mixing bowl combine flour and salt. Cut in butter until mixture is the size of small peas.

2. Sprinkle 1 tablespoon of water over part of mixture, gently toss with fork. Repeat until all is moistened. Form dough into ball. On lightly floured surface, flatten dough into disc, wrap with plastic, and refrigerate until ready to use, or for 30 minutes.

3. Roll dough into 12" circle. Unroll onto pie plate being careful not to stretch pastry. Trim edges to ½" beyond the edge of pie plate; fold under extra pastry.

4. Make a fluted edge by using the back of a fork and pressing evenly around the edges. Bake as directed in recipe.

Pie Filling

- 1 stick butter, melted and cooled
- 1½ cups premium white chocolate morsels
- 3 TB. flour
- 1¼ cups sugar
- 4 eggs, whisked
- 1 cup buttermilk
- 1½ tsp. vanilla
- 1 TB. lemon juice, fresh squeezed
- 1 TB. lemon zest
- Pinch of grated nutmeg

1. Preheat oven to 425°F.

2. Slowly melt together butter and chocolate chip morsels. Set aside to cool.

3. In mixer, combine flour and sugar.

4. Stir in eggs and buttermilk.

5. Add cooled melted butter/white chocolate mixture, vanilla, lemon juice, and lemon zest.

6. Add a pinch-or-two of grated nutmeg.

7. Pour into pie crust.

8. Put pie in center of oven and bake at 425°F for 15 minutes, then lower to 350°F, and bake for 40 minutes.

9. Cool, then keep chilled.

Raspberry Sauce

- 1 pint fresh raspberries
- ¼ cup white sugar
- 2 TB. orange juice
- 2 TB. cornstarch
- 1 cup cold water

1. Combine raspberries, sugar, and orange juice in saucepan.

2. In separate bowl, whisk cornstarch into cold water until smooth. Add mixture to sauce pan and bring to boil.

3. Simmer for about 5 minutes, stirring constantly, until the sauce thickens. It will further thicken as it cools.

4. Purée sauce in blender, or with handheld immersion blender, and strain through fine sieve.

5. Drizzle sauce over pie slices immediately before serving.

NANCY SORIANO

Nancy Soriano is an editorial strategist who has worked in media and publishing for twenty years. Passionate about design, handmade, and lifestyle, Nancy is an innovative thinker and collaborator who can develop and diversify brands and businesses for today's consumer market in both print and digital media.

Nancy was the editor-in-chief of *Country Living* magazine for ten years, with a monthly circulation of 1.6 million readers, where she built the magazine into a multi-platform brand. In 2009, Nancy went on to co-found, with Jo Packham, The Creative Connection, a three-day crafting, social media, and business conference that celebrates creative women and women entrepreneurs. Recently, Nancy was Community Leader|Publishing Director for Craft at F+W Media.

Nancy is a frequent guest on *Good Morning America* and *Martha Stewart* Sirius Radio, as well as a speaker at Etsy and VK Live. Today, she is a media and brand consultant for media, publishing, and design companies.

An avid home cook who can usually be found baking in her kitchen weekend mornings and preparing for Sunday night dinner with family and friends, Nancy lives with her husband, son, and dog Violet in a 1924 Tudor cottage. For more about Nancy, visit Nancysoriano.com.

When Jo asked me to participate in this book I was overjoyed. I love the concept of
Pieography. I spent days asking myself (and husband) what pie represents me: which one
would it be? At first I thought of fruit pies since my mom often baked them (she made
a fabulous apple pie). But that seemed too singular and more about my memories of
growing up. What pie tells my story? Represents who I am, where I have been? It was a
wonderful assignment that required more self-reflection than I anticipated. I'm still not
sure if my choice of Banana Cream Pie with Chocolate and Caramel fully represents all
of who I am and the experiences that have shaped me. But, I do think it brings together
and captures key components of what I value and aspire towards: comfort, classic design,
timeless traditions, layered complex experiences, all mixed with personal style.

For me, banana cream pie is a classic comfort food, and comfort is key to who I am.
When made with quality, natural ingredients, that first taste of pie is like sinking into
the most comfortable sofa … you just relax and let go. It feels like home. Your mouth
says comfort. Banana cream pie is classic and traditional. Always appropriate for any
occasion, and never out of place, it's really just a question of when you want to serve
it. It forever speaks to our hearts, as traditions usually do. I mix classic and traditional
design in my own home, yet I like to put my personal style and stamp upon them. In this
recipe, the "stamp" would be the crust. Rather than a traditional graham cracker crust, I
make a flaky pastry crust, of butter and vegetable shortening (which is what my mother
used). The complexity of the pie (or, of myself) is reflected in the layering of flavors: the
chocolate ganache and caramel sauce, hidden below, discovered only when a person
has tasted the pie. As in most aspects of life, there is more than meets the eye. This
component adds just the right touch of complexity, with familiar flavors, and a welcomed
surprise. And, of course, quality of the ingredients, as in all things, is key in bringing the
flavors (and look) to life.

We are what we eat, so we are told. Food tells a story and reflects our experiences and
emotions: when life throws us a curve ball or when we hit a home run. And what better
way to enjoy and reflect on life than with a slice of pie.

Banana Cream Pie with Chocolate & Caramel

makes one 10-inch pie, inspired by Tartine

Flaky Pie Crust

- 1 tsp. salt
- ⅔ cup very cold water
- 3 cups + 2 TB. flour
- ½ cup chilled butter, cut into 1-inch cubes
- ½ cup vegetable shortening (Crisco), cut into chunks

1. Dissolve salt in water and keep cold.

2. To make dough with a food processor: put flour in work bowl, place butter and shortening over flour, and pulse until mixture forms crumbs, the size of peas. Add salted water and pulse for several seconds, until dough comes together as a ball, but is not completely smooth. (You want to see pieces of butter/shortening.)

3. On floured surface, divide dough into 2 balls, shape into a 1" thick disk, wrap in plastic wrap, and chill for at least 2 hours or up to overnight.

4. Preheat oven to 375°F.

5. Roll out one disk on a lightly floured surface to ⅛" thick. Transfer dough round to pie dish, placing and pressing into place. Trim edges. Line with parchment paper and pie weights or dry beans.

6. Bake until surface looks dry, about 20 minutes. Remove from oven and remove parchment and weights or beans and return shell to oven for another 3–5 minutes. If center starts to rise, gently pierce with a fork or knife. Let cool completely.

Chocolate Ganache

- 1 10 oz. bittersweet chocolate, broken in pieces
- 1 cup heavy cream

Place chocolate pieces into bowl. Heat heavy cream to boiling point and pour over chocolate. Let stand a couple of minutes and carefully stir until fully incorporated and glossy. Cool to room temperature. Pour over cooled pastry shell and refrigerate.

Salted Butter Caramel Sauce

- 1½ cups sugar
- ¼ cup light corn syrup
- ¼ cup water
- 1 cup heavy cream
- 5 TB. salted butter, cut into pieces

1. In heavy-bottomed saucepan combine sugar, corn syrup, and water over medium-low heat until sugar dissolves. Increase heat and bring to boil, without stirring. Use wet pastry brush or silicon spatula to wash down any crystals on sides of pan. Boil until syrup is deep amber color, about 5–6 minutes.

2. Remove sugar from heat and carefully whisk in heavy cream. Mixture will bubble.

3. Stir in salted butter. Mix well.

4. Cool. Drizzle over chocolate in pie shell to cover completely. You will have caramel sauce left over.

Pastry Cream

- 2 cups whole milk
- 1 tsp. vanilla
- ¼ tsp. salt
- ¾ cup sugar
- 4 TB. cornstarch
- 2 large eggs
- 4 TB. butter, cut in small cubes
- 2 ripe bananas, sliced
- Chocolate shavings, for decoration

1. Heat milk, vanilla, and salt in pan over medium heat, and bring to boil.

2. In large mixing bowl, whisk sugar, cornstarch, and eggs until blended. Slowly add half of milk mixture into egg and whisk constantly to temper them. Add remaining milk and then return all of it to saucepan.

3. Cook until a thick custard consistency, whisking continuously. Remove from heat and pour into bowl.

4. Let cool for 10 minutes. After 10 minutes, mix in butter, 1 tablespoon at a time, until mixture is smooth.

5. Cover surface with plastic wrap, directly touching cream. Cool completely.

6. Layer half of pastry cream on top of chocolate and caramel pie shell.

7. Arrange bananas over cream. Cover bananas with remaining cream.

8. Finish with chocolate shavings on top.

9. If you have extra caramel sauce, you can drizzle over pie slices when serving.

KELLY STERLING

Kelly works as a professionally trained chef, food photographer, and stylist. She says her approach to food is best summed up in these few words: *Keep it simple, natural, and beautiful.*

Kelly's life revolves around food, and always has. Her father was a pastry chef who taught her that practice makes perfect. Her mother owned and operated a few restaurants while she was growing up, and Kelly credits her mom with teaching her how to hustle in a busy kitchen, use dangerous equipment, and serve everyone a pretty plate of food, even if it's meatloaf. Kelly's grandmother taught her how to grow a garden, even in the most challenging conditions (imagine the Arizona desert, in the summer). Her grandfather taught her how to be a good eater, and how much joy can come from a simple meal shared with family and friends. From a young age, Kelly learned what real food looks, feels, smells, and tastes like.

Kelly splits her time between San Francisco and Miami with her husband and adorable little dog, Bailey. To learn more about Kelly, visit www.kellysterling.com and her blog, www.snailsview.com.

If my life were a pie, it would be a Classic Lemon Pie with Poached and Toasted Meringue and Chambord-Spiked Berries: simple, yet complex, and made with love. I have an old soul (classic lemon pie) with the curiosity of a child (toasted meringue is like toasting marshmallows over an open fire). I cherish tradition (family and friends) what's always worked (classic recipes), yet I seek out the new and unique with both ingredients and techniques (poached meringue, Chambord berries).

I'm soulful, grounded, and easy going. I like to dig in the dirt. But at the same time I'm high end, classy, fussy, and very much a perfectionist. The single thing that defines me in EVERY area of my life—from cooking to relationships—is LOVE. My love expresses itself through food, friendship, family, and life itself. I love food enough to respect it and treat it with reverence, joy, and honor. I do the same with people. I see them as their highest selves. I honor, accept, and treasure them. I offer my ear, my food, my wisdom, and myself with great love to everyone around me.

Classic Lemon Pie

I bring out the best of life; I bring out the best ingredients. My surroundings are simple, as are my ingredients—fresh, natural, and beautiful. It doesn't get much simpler than fresh eggs, cream, sugar, and lemons. When I think of a classic lemon pie, I automatically think of all its possibilities, beyond what others see. I do the same with people. You may think of a lemon pie as familiar, but because I see it as an old soul, my lemon pie becomes: simple yet complex, traditional but unique, and familiar with unexpected twists. This pie is me.

Poached and Toasted Meringue

This meringue smells like marshmallows roasting over an open fire. Though I cherish and keep what's best from the past, I think of myself like a child who sees the world brand new, fascinating, and wondrous every day. I have a great sense of play; nothing is so sacred that I won't see other possibilities for it. Just as a kid sees a magic wand in a stick, or a Superman cape in an old blanket, I see possibilities everywhere. I don't just look for the unique, I create it. Why bake the meringue when I can gently poach it?

Chambord-spiked Berries

These are like summer in a bowl, bright and fresh. I could have left the berries natural, but I knew they could be even better. I gently bathe them in a touch of Chambord, sugar, lemon, and homemade vanilla extract that was given to me by a cherished dear friend.
I will feed my pie to the people I cherish, whom in turn will feed me.

Classic Lemon Pie with Poached-Toasted Meringue & Chambord-Spiked Berries

makes one 9-inch tart

Chambord-Spiked Berries

- ½ pint blueberries, rinsed
- 1 pint strawberries, rinsed and cut in half or quarters
- ½ lemon, juice and zest
- 2 TB. sugar
- 1 TB. Chambord
- ¼ tsp. vanilla extract (or pulp from ¼ bean)

1. Combine all ingredients in a bowl. Gently toss together. Let sit at least 1 hour or up to 1 day in refrigerator.

Lemon Filling

- 6 eggs, room temperature
- 1 cup sugar
- 1 cup fresh lemon juice
- 1½ organic lemons, zested
- ⅛ tsp. sea salt
- ¾ cup heavy cream
- 1 recipe pâte sucrée

1. Mix together eggs, sugar, and lemon juice (be careful not to foam it up too much) until sugar is dissolved. Strain.

2. Stir in lemon zest, salt, and cream until well blended. Refrigerate.

3. Before serving, skim off any bubbles or foam that may have surfaced, which will assure a beautiful, glossy-finished pie.

Pâte Sucrée and Assembly

makes one 9-inch crust

- 1 cup all-purpose flour
- 2 TB. sugar
- ⅛ tsp. sea salt
- 4 oz. unsalted butter, chilled and cut into small pieces
- 1 large egg yolk
- 1 TB. heavy cream or milk

1. Using food processor or stand mixer, combine flour, sugar, and salt. Add butter and process until mixture resembles coarse meal.

2. Whisk together egg yolk and cream. With machine running, slowly pour them in. When all is added, pulse a few more times until dough comes together. If it's too dry, add more cream, 1 teaspoon at a time. Wrap in plastic and refrigerate for at least 1 hour.

3. Roll Pâte Sucrée out on a floured surface and transfer to pie pan. (Reserve a small piece of dough for patching.) Chill for at least 30 minutes.

4. Preheat oven to 350°F.

5. Once chilled, line with parchment paper and fill with pie weights or beans. Place in center of oven and bake for 20 minutes or until golden brown. Carefully remove parchment and weights. With reserved dough, patch any cracks that may have formed in crust. Return to oven and cook until it's a rich brown (more color means more flavor). Cooking time will vary depending on how thick it's rolled out.

6. When done, remove from oven and cool on wire rack. Lower oven temperature to 275°F. When pie shell has cooled, return to middle of oven directly on rack. Pour in lemon filling, using something with a pour spout. (Filling the pie this way keeps you from spilling it on the way to the oven, resulting in a soggy crust and messy floor!) Bake for 30–35 minutes, or until pie has a firm jiggle. Also, pie will continue to cook a little once removed from oven. Oven temperatures vary, so keep a close eye on pie during last few minutes of cooking. Let cool to room temperature, add meringue before serving.

Poached Meringue

    1½ cup whole milk
    1½ cup water
    8 oz. egg whites, room temperature
    3 TB. powdered sugar, sifted
    ½ cup sugar

1. Pour milk and water into large shallow pan (the largest one you have). Turn to moderate heat and bring just to a simmer. Turn to low while you prepare meringue.

2. Pull out slotted spoon, ice cream scoop (with a thumb release), and sheet pan lined with paper towels.

3. In bowl of a stand mixer (or using hand mixer), pour in egg whites and turn to low until foamy, just a few seconds. Add powdered sugar and mix to soft peaks. Add sugar all at once. Turn mixer to high speed and mix for about 30 seconds to form firm peaks. Be careful not to overmix meringue. It will fall apart when you add it to simmering milk.

4. Working quickly, place heaping scoops of meringue into simmering milk mixture. Scoop as many as will fit comfortably without crowding, leaving room to flip them over. (You may need to do this in two batches.)

5. Cook 2 minutes per side and remove onto paper towels. Let cool in the refrigerator until use. Place 1 ball of meringue on each slice of lemon tart. Toast meringue with a torch just before serving. Add berries.

155

SALLI SWINDELL

Salli Swindell and Nate Padavick are a brother/sister design and illustration team known as Studio SSS. Together they have designed thousands of greeting cards, patterns, magazine and book illustrations for clients such as Pottery Barn, American Greetings, Jo Ann Stores, Inc., and Great Arrow Graphics. They are the founders of They Draw & Cook and They Draw & Travel. Both websites feature the amazing talents of thousands of artists from around the world through illustrated recipes and maps. Salli and Nate agree that when things become a little stressful they both like to do the same thing to relax: illustrate recipes and maps! Their first book was released in October 2011.

Check out theydrawandcook.com and theydrawandtravel.com for a new perspective on food and travel and maybe even think about submitting a recipe or map of your own. Both sites frequently host contests sponsored by the likes of Food Network, All Recipes and Pentel. The collective energy on both sites is contagious and there is always something new happening!

My life & Espresso Dream Pie

Layer by layer, flavor by flavor my life is every bit as sweet, smooth, and delicious as my Espresso Dream Pie. I chose a cream pie because my life has evolved into a very well blended mix of family, friends and creativity, all infused with lots of fun. Although the main ingredients are vanilla, espresso, chocolate, and orange zest you can change it up to accommodate your tastes. Maybe try coconut or hazelnuts? That's a big part of how I live my life; I try something, see how it feels, and if it's not quite right I make adjustments.

My childhood was very much like a dollop of vanilla whipped cream, comforting and uncomplicated, with just the right amount of sweetness, like a hug from grandma. There are so many things about my life that leave me feeling as rich as the finest chocolate. If you could see me and my siblings and all of our families pile into a beach house every summer for vacation, you would immediately sense my crazy and wonderful joy!

The most prevailing flavor in my pie might just be the espresso. I AM espresso! I always wake up ready to greet another day of possibilities. My best and most creative work is done before 10 a.m., then it's time for coffee round two. My brother and studio partner Nate and I seem to manage our business through caffeinated video chats and morning e-mails.

And what better way to describe the bright and surprising moments of my life than with a sprinkling of orange zest! Whether it be a funny story from one of our boys, an awesome recipe submission to They Draw & Cook, a newly discovered color palette, or the adorableness of one of our cats perched on my husbands shoulders, every single day has a zesty sparkle that never fails to delight me. While this may not be the simplest of pies to make, it surely reflects that every good life is full of generous amounts of work, mindfulness, espresso, and laughter.

157

Espresso Dream Pie

makes one 9-inch pie

Pie Crust

 2 cups chocolate wafers, crushed

 ¼ cup sugar

 6 TB. butter, melted

1. Preheat oven to 325°F.

2. Combine wafers, sugar, butter, and press into 9" buttered pie dish, making sure to cover all sides.

3. Bake for 10 minutes.

Pie Filling

 ¾ cup sugar

 ¼ cup cornstarch

 ¼ tsp. salt

 2½ cups whole milk

 2 TB. instant espresso powder

 4 egg yolks

 ¼ cup coffee liqueur

 1 tsp. vanilla extract

 4 TB. unsalted butter, softened

1. Combine sugar, cornstarch, and salt in medium saucepan.

2. Whisk in milk and espresso powder, cook over medium high heat, stirring constantly until bubbly and thick (about 7 minutes). Continue stirring and cook about 2 more minutes.

3. Whisk yolks together in separate bowl. Slowly pour milk mixture into bowl of yolks while whisking entire time.

4. Return to saucepan and continue to cook until it reaches a boil, stirring constantly (about 1–2 minutes).

5. Remove from heat and stir in coffee liqueur and vanilla.

6. Add 1 tablespoon of butter at a time. Let mixture cool in saucepan on wire rack for about 10 minutes, whisking occasionally.

7. Pour custard into wafer crust and cover with plastic wrap (letting wrap completely touch the custard). Refrigerate at least 4 hours.

Pie Topping

 ¾ cup heavy cream

 1 TB. sugar

 1 tsp. vanilla

 ½ orange, zested

 Dark chocolate shavings

1. Right before serving pie, beat cream, sugar, and vanilla to form stiff peaks.

2. Generously coat top of pie and sprinkle with finely grated zest of half an orange.

3. Finish with shavings of dark chocolate.

KORALEE TEICHROEB

Creating has always been a part of Koralee Teichroeb's life. As a young girl she spent hours around her Grandma's kitchen table baking, crafting, and collecting.

Today Koralee's world is dusted with everything from glitter to cake sprinkles. You can usually find her in her kitchen with her camera, as her creative side has now discovered the JOYS of photography. Koralee's baking and photographs may be found in the pages of *Where Women Cook*, where she fills her column "Joy Making Days" with yummy treats and ideas to share with those you love.

Her latest adventure is her book, *Everything Goes with Ice Cream*, a collection of heavenly bites and charming bits which will hit the bookshelves soon.

Koralee's photographs, paired with her little bits of daily wisdom, can be found on her creative blog Bluebird Notes, www.bluebirdnotes.blogspot.com, where she shows us that it is the "little things in life" that truly matter the most.

My life & Baked Raspberry Pink Meringue Pie

Raspberries, sweet raspberries, little bundles of joy. My pie would have to be filled with these little parcels of pure goodness. My pie, like my life, is filled with many sweet blessings—oodles of little joys, like raspberries.

Of course, not every day is filled with sweetness. Just like the berries in my pie, not every berry is perfectly sweet, plump, and juicy. There are some small sour ones and old mushy ones. I cannot possibly pick out every bad berry before I make my pie; I know the bad ones will cook up with the sweet juicy ones, and my pie will taste amazing even with the bad ones still in. Just like life, the bad days get absorbed by the good days when you take time to focus on the blessings all around you. There's always more to be thankful for than not. Finding the joys makes for one incredibly sweet life.

A rich chocolate crust combines perfectly with sweet raspberries. My life is rich in spirituality, the foundation I live and grow by. If I did not have my feet planted firmly on rich spiritual ground, it would be hard for me to recognize these blessings and joys of mine. Spirituality and blessings go hand in hand, just like the firm pie crust that holds the juicy berries in place.

What would life be like without a little bit of whimsical fun—hence the pink meringue topping! I am happiest when surrounded by soft pinks, an oh-so-sweet girly color that makes my world fanciful and fun. I love using my imagination to bring smiles to the faces around me. And a raspberry pie topped with mile-high fluffy PINK meringue: now if that doesn't make you smile, nothing will!

Baked Raspberry Pink Meringue Pie with Rich Chocolate Crust

makes one 9-inch pie

Pie Crust

makes two 9" pie crusts (you will have 1 left over)

- 2 cups flour
- ½ cup sugar
- 3 TB. cocoa powder
- ½ tsp. salt
- 8 TB. cold unsalted butter, cut into small cubes
- 4 egg yolks
- ½ tsp. vanilla extract

1. Into large mixing bowl, sift together flour, sugar, cocoa powder, and salt.

2. Using pastry blender, mix in butter until mixture is crumbly.

3. Stir in egg yolks and vanilla until mixture is moist.

4. Turn dough out onto work surface and knead until dough clings together and becomes smooth (about 2 minutes).

5. Form into a disk then wrap in plastic, chill at least 30 minutes or overnight.

Tips: This pie dough is very soft and must be handled carefully. It easily falls apart when rolling out. I recommend that you roll it out thinly between 2 sheets of parchment paper. Chill dough once it is made, and then again after it is shaped in the pie plate.

Pie Filling

- 4 cups raspberries, fresh or frozen (If frozen berries are used, let them thaw in a colander first; otherwise pie might be runny.)
- ½ cup sugar
- ½ cup flour

1. Preheat oven to 350°F.

2. Carefully mix 3½ cups of berries with sugar and flour.

3. Spread on top of chilled prepared pie crust.

4. Spread remaining ½ cup berries on top.

5. Bake for 5–7 minutes, then add tin foil rim or rim cover around edges so crust does not burn. Because this crust in already dark before baking, it will darken even more. Continue baking for 25 minutes until top is bubbly.

6. Remove and let cool before adding meringue topping.

Pink Meringue

- 8 large egg whites
- ⅔ cup sugar
- ¼ tsp. salt
- Pink food coloring

1. Preheat oven to 350°F.

2. Combine egg whites, sugar, and salt in a mixing bowl; beat until stiff peaks are formed.

3. Add food coloring a little at a time until desired shade is achieved. Remember you can always add more but can't take any away. Very little is needed to achieve a soft pink color. Do not overbeat egg whites.

4. Spoon meringue on top of raspberry pie, making sure it is piled all the way around and touches the crust. To make soft peaks use back of a spoon.

5. Bake until meringue peaks are golden brown, 7–9 minutes. If you feel crust is getting too brown, cover with foil.

6. Let pie cool before cutting. Pie is best if served on the same day.

Debbee Thibault

Debbee Thibault grew up in sunny Southern California and credits the person she is today to "a truly wonderful childhood." She's always been interested in old toys and folk art, probably because of the historic neighborhood she lived in as a child. She says, "Older folks would take us under their wings, to teach us and tell us stories about the past. I became fascinated by the antiques that lined their walls, along with the way they decorated their homes."

In the 1970s, her teen years, Debbee and her friend designed their own fashions. They made bathing suits and beach clothes out of old materials and sold them to local vintage clothing stores.

While married and raising two children, Debbee continued to stay creative, working with Neiman Marcus in the 1980s, making Christmas ornaments out of bread dough.

Inspired by the old toys and interests of her childhood, Debbee tried her hand at paper mâché, designing toy-like figures and holiday-themed items similar to mâché pieces created long ago. Others encouraged her to turn her craft into a business, and she did just that. Visit www.debbeethibault.com to learn more about Debbee's charming creations.

1. You might say that my somewhat made-up apple pie recipe started out as nothing
2. and became something. I don't have any highfalutin words to describe this pie, but it
3. is curious and interesting like me, not to mention the melt-in-your-mouth absolutely
4. scrumdiddlyumtious taste. Most of my friends and family who have tried a tantalizing
5. morsel beg for more!
6.
7. Years ago I would have never guessed my profession to be a paper mâché artist who makes a
8. living at designing toy-like creations and funky jewelry. I found great joy in making things out
9. of ordinary materials in my childhood and, much like the pie, my career started with paper.
10. The paper grocery bag is the key to my pie process. For starters, when my day is harried, a
11. frozen Pet Milk pie shell does the trick. This particular brand has a wonderful homemade
12. buttery flavor, but your own favorite pie shell recipe will do if you have time. I love fresh
13. produce, and apples are one of my favorites when it comes to fruit. I love the flavor of tart
14. apples, and prefer Granny Smith. Basting and tossing the apples with the lemon juice and
15. combined dry ingredients creates a savory flavor when the baking is complete.
16.
17. I've lived an interesting life with a combination of ups and downs. I have been through the
18. school of hard knocks and hopefully I have become a richer and wiser person for it. At ease
19. with the passing of time, and now comfortable in my shoes, SAVORY seems like a fitting
20. word for the fullness that I live. I am also sweet, spicy, playful, mischievous, and even a little
21. nutty at times.
22.
23. When making this delicious filling and trying to stay current with the times, I might change
24. the recipe a bit by adding something new or subtracting an element or two. Somehow it all
25. comes together consistently, much like me. The buttery topping is very simple … I find that
26. the things in life that touch me the most are simple; once I combine the butter and flour
27. with a pinch of salt, I melt the items on the stove while stirring with a wooden spoon. I pat
28. the melted topping onto the savory coated apples and add a decorative touch of nuts for the
29. taste and looks. The pie is now ready to slip into the brown paper grocery bag.
30.

Fold the top of the bag down, and then paperclip securely to seal in the juices. I let the pie
bake and simmer for one hour, checking the oven from time to time, making sure it doesn't
burn. Let the pie cool and add a dollop of fresh homemade whipping cream. As they say:
voilá … like magic, from humble to happening … I guess that's me!

Brown Bag Apple Pie

makes one 9-inch deep dish pie

¼ cup granulated sugar (You may prefer more sugar depending on tartness of apples.)

2 TB. flour, well rounded

1 tsp. cinnamon

¼ tsp. nutmeg

½ cup + 2 TB. walnuts, chopped

6–8 Granny Smith apples, peeled and sliced

1–2 TB. lemon juice (varies by sweetness of apples)

1 deep dish Pet Milk pie shell, or other pastry shell

1 brown paper grocery bag

2 paper clips

Topping

1 stick butter

⅔ cup flour

1 tsp. salt

½ cup sugar

Note: You may need a little more flour or sugar depending on consistency or taste.)

Whipping cream

1. Preheat oven to 350°F.

2. In mixing bowl, combine sugar, flour, cinnamon, nutmeg, and ½ cup walnuts.

3. Toss mixture over apples and squeeze in lemon juice, making sure apples are well coated.

4. Spoon into deep dish pie shell and set aside.

5. In pan over low heat, melt butter carefully so that it doesn't burn.

6. In separate bowl, combine flour, salt, and sugar. Stir mixture into melted butter. You may add more flour or sugar depending on taste.

7. Pat buttery topping onto apples, covering them well.

8. Add 2 tablespoons walnuts creating a circle on top of pie for a creative and appetizing touch.

9. Place pie into paper bag and fold ends. Clip with paper clips. This will seal in juices. Remove top rack from oven and place bag in center of rack, making sure not to touch heated rods. Bake for 1 hour.

10. Add a dollop of fresh whipped cream for finishing touch.

CAUTION: The bag may smell like it is burning as pie bakes. Always check to make sure that the pie is centered properly and continue to bake.

VIRGINIA WILLIS

Virginia Willis has cooked Lapin Normandie with Julia Child, prepared lunch for President Clinton, and catered a bowling party for Jane Fonda. She began her culinary career tossing pizzas in college, and has since foraged for wild herbs in the Alps, made mustard in Dijon, crushed olives in California, and harvested capers in the shadow of a smoldering volcano in Sicily. Her first job in a professional kitchen was as an apprentice for Nathalie Dupree's TV cooking show on PBS. Willis has subsequently produced over a tousand TV episodes, working for Martha Stewart, Bobby Flay, and Epicurious on the Discovery Channel.

Her critically acclaimed cookbook *Bon Appétit, Y'all: Recipes and Stories from Three Generations of Southern Cooking* was "rated the number one comfort food book of 2008" by the *Chicago Tribune*. Her latest book, *Basic to Brilliant Y'all: 150 Refined Southern Recipes and Ways to Dress Them Up for Company*, was rated one of the best cookbooks of 2011 by FOX News. She was an editor for *The All-New Joy of Cooking*; author of *Pasta Dinners 1, 2, 3*; and an editorial assistant to Anne Willan for *Cook It Right*. Her articles have appeared in *Country Living*, *Family Fun*, and *Eating Well*. She is also the founder and owner of My Southern Pantry, a specialty artisan food line featuring heirloom organic grits, cornmeal, smoked salts, and spices.

For more about Virginia and to read her popular blog, please visit www.virginiawillis.com.

My life as a pie would undoubtedly be Aunt Julia's Chocolate Pie. This family recipe starts with a traditional all-American crust. My life has a classic foundation built on tight family bonds. I enjoyed the Southern version of an all-American childhood. Summers were spent spitting watermelon seeds off the back steps with my sister and cousins, fishing for bream at our pond with my grandparents, and learning how to swim with Mama in the shallow waves at the beach. I remember my mother proudly announcing one night during dinner while I was in second grade that I was going to be a Girl Scout Brownie. My heart fills with joy at the memory. I recall my exuberance and excitement as if it were yesterday. (I remained a Girl Scout throughout my childhood into adolescence, finishing at the Senior level.)

On top of the buttery, flaky crust of Aunt Julia's Chocolate Pie is a rich chocolate filling that is prepared country-style, with a full range of flavor. My life is complex and multifaceted with diverse experiences and emotions. I am Southern-born and French-trained. I grew up on a red dirt road, yet have traveled in nearly a dozen countries and visited 49 of the 50 states.

I am happy, blessed, and thankful in my rich life. My work is full and different every day, with plentiful new faces in person and online, and abundant opportunities to experience new things. I have sweet love in my life and longtime dear friends, one of the best being my mother. Yet not all is simply sweet. I often think "too sweet" is flat and one-dimensional. The pudding in Aunt Julia's Chocolate Pie has a gentle bitterness, not enough to be unpleasant, but just enough to let you know it's there. I, like most, have lived, loved, and lost. Not enough to be unpleasant, but just enough to make me appreciate my blessings along with my challenges.

Lastly, Aunt Julia's Chocolate Pie is topped with a pompadour of lightly toasted golden meringue. The combination of the flaky buttery crust, the chocolate cream, and the eggy meringue is classic, old-fashioned, country, and French-inspired, all in one. Just like me; just like my life.

Aunt Julia's Chocolate Pie

makes one 9-inch pie, Adapted from *Bon Appétit, Y'all: Recipes and Stories from Three Generations of Southern Cooking* by Virginia Willis

All-American Pie Crust

makes one 9-inch pie crust

- 1¼ cups all-purpose flour, plus more for rolling
- ½ tsp. fine sea salt
- ¼ cup solid vegetable shortening, preferably Crisco, chilled and cut into pieces
- 4 TB. unsalted butter, chilled and cut into pieces
- 3–8 TB. ice water

1. In work bowl of food processor fitted with metal blade, combine flour and salt, then add vegetable shortening and butter. Process until mixture resembles coarse meal, 8–10 seconds.

2. With processor on pulse, add enough ice water, 1 tablespoon at a time, until dough holds together without being sticky or crumbly. Shape dough into a disk and wrap in plastic wrap. Chill until firm and moisture has distributed evenly, about 30 minutes.

3. Flour clean work surface and rolling pin. Place dough disk in center of floured surface. Starting in center of dough, roll to, but not over, upper edge of dough. Return to center, and roll down to, but not over, lower edge. Lift dough, give it a quarter turn, and lay it on work surface. Continue rolling, repeating quarter turns, until you have a disk about ⅛" thick.

4. Ease pastry into 9" pie plate. Trim 1" larger than diameter of pie plate; fold overhanging pastry under itself along rim of plate. For a simple decorative edge, press tines of a fork around folded pastry. To make a fluted edge, using both your finger and thumb, pinch and crimp folded dough. Chill until firm, about 30 minutes.

5. Heat oven to 425°F.

6. Crumple piece of parchment and place it over pie. Weight paper with pie weights or dried beans. This will keep pie crust from bubbling up. Bake until deep golden brown, 25–30 minutes. Remove paper and weights.

Pie Filling and Assembly

- 1 cup sugar
- 2 cups whole milk, divided
- 3½ TB. all-purpose flour
- ¼ cup cocoa powder
- 3 large eggs, separated
- ½ tsp. pure vanilla extract
- Pinch of fine sea salt
- 1 tsp. cream of tartar
- 2 TB. powdered sugar

1. Preheat oven to 500°F.

2. To prepare pie filling, in saucepan, combine sugar and 1 cup of milk. Set aside.

3. In bowl, combine remaining 1 cup milk, flour, and cocoa powder and whisk thoroughly to combine. (Mama uses a shaker and shakes the mixture until it is well combined and frothy.) Set aside.

4. Heat milk-sugar mixture in saucepan over medium-high heat until simmering. Slowly add milk-flour mixture and stir to combine. Bring to boil. Add egg yolks, whisking constantly, until it returns to boil. Once mixture comes to boil, immediately add vanilla and remove from heat.

5. Pour mixture into fully baked pie crust. Set aside.

6. To make meringue topping, place egg whites in bowl with pinch of salt. Add cream of tartar, using handheld mixer whisk on high speed until foamy. Sift over powdered sugar a little at a time and whisk until whites are glossy and hold stiff peaks when whisk is lifted.

7. To finish pie, spoon meringue over pie, making sure it touches edges of pie crust. Bake until golden brown, 3–5 minutes. Move to a rack to cool completely and set. Serve.

Additional Photography Provided By:

Lauryn Byrdy pg. 94
Samantha Cabrera pg. 140, 142–143
Anita Chu pg. 72–73
Julie Cove pg. 75–77
Ryne Hazen pg. 8, 36, 85

Tiffany Kirchner-Dixon pg. 52, 54–55
Angie Mosier pg. 168
Jen O'Connor pg. 62, 118, 120–121
Carolyn Robb pg. 133, 135

Laurie Schneider Photography pg. 126
Koralee Teichroeb pg. 160, 163
Zachary Williams pg. 82

conversions & equivalents

Metric Conversion Chart by Volume
(for Liquids)

U.S.	Metric (milliliters/liters)
1/4 teaspoon	1.25 mL
1/2 teaspoon	2.5 mL
1 teaspoon	5 mL
1 tablespoon	15 mL
1/4 cup	60 mL
1/2 cup	120 mL
3/4 cup	180 mL
1 cup	240 mL
2 cups (1 pint)	480 mL
4 cups (1 quart)	960 mL
4 quarts (1 gallon)	3.8 L

Metric Conversion Chart by Weight
(for Dry Ingredients)

U.S.	Metric (grams/kilograms)
1/4 teaspoon	1 g
1/2 teaspoon	2 g
1 teaspoon	5 g
1 tablespoon	15 g
16 ounces (1 pound)	450 g
2 pounds	900 g
3 pounds	1.4 kg
4 pounds	1.8 kg
5 pounds	2.3 kg
6 pounds	2.7 kg

Temperature Conversion

Fahrenheit	Celsius
32°	0°
212°	100°
250°	121°
275°	135°
300°	149°
350°	177°
375°	191°
400°	204°
425°	218°

Cooking Measurement Equivalents

3 teaspoons = 1 tablespoon

2 tablespoons = 1 fluid ounce

4 tablespoons = 1/4 cup

5 tablespoons + 1 teaspoon = 1/3 cup

8 tablespoons = 1/2 cup

10 tablespoons + 2 teaspoons = 2/3 cup

12 tablespoons = 3/4 cup

16 tablespoons = 1 cup

48 teaspoons = 1 cup

1 cup = 8 fluid ounces

2 cups = 1 pint

2 pints = 1 quart

4 quarts = 1 gallon

Index

I made
for you a Pie...

Krys Kirpatrick
Hutch Studio